I Used to be Gifted:

Understanding and Nurturing Gifted Learners at Home and in the Classroom

Mark Hess

Gifted
UNLIMITED

Edited by: William D. Beuscher
Interior design: The Printed Page
Cover design: Kelly Crimi

Published by
Gifted Unlimited, LLC
12340 U.S. Highway 42, No. 453
Goshen, KY 40026
www.giftedunlimitedllc.com

ISBN: 978-1-953360-16-8

For my own gifted kids, Kinsey and Zachary,
and for those hundreds and thousands of gifted kids
who have brought so much joy to my life over the years.
And to Susie who helped me understand this teacher
is who I am and always will be.

Table of Contents

Introduction

Please allow me to introduce myself. I may be your second favorite teacher. Hayden, a first grader, once told me that…and first graders know stuff. They know things that we adults have long ago forgotten.

Hayden will be a senior in high school next year. I may have slipped down his list a little bit. I may be number nineteen now if you don't count custodians.

One time at a faculty meeting it was suggested that I supervise a particularly difficult grade's lunch recess. I was unfairly accused of being really good at recess duty. Late in the day in faculty meetings when everyone is ready to go home is a time we teachers become susceptible to wild errors in judgement. I'm the sort of teacher who has trouble keeping a really tight and orderly line as my students wind their way through the hallways, and I probably only survive because other teachers have done the groundwork with their kids before I got hold of them. One year, it was my duty to walk the kindergartners to the bus every day after school. That line was really a mess. But I did discover that I was really good at holding hands. Boys and girls alike fought for that coveted spot holding my hands at the back of the line. One time, with a student holding each hand on either side of me, a third little girl swept in and karate chopped her classmate's hand away from mine. I must note that this was inappropriate behavior, but I will also note that it may have been one of the most validating moments I've had in my teaching career. Plus, we love bold and assertive girls, don't we?

In the spring of 1997, I was the athletics and activities director in a small school district at the foot of Pikes Peak, having been a high school English and speech teacher and coach for the previous

9 years. The district's elementary school gifted resource teacher was about to leave to a new city at spring break, and I asked to fill her vacancy. With two young children at home, as well as the late nights and conflicts of an activities director, I was beginning to realize my dislike of interscholastic sports, which I had never wanted to be involved with in the first place. I thought, however, that I could readily relate to gifted kids. For the rest of the school year, I held down both positions. It was the best professional decision I have ever made.

Although I didn't know it at the time, I had already been introduced to the ground floor of gifted education. George Betts at the University of Northern Colorado is one of gifted education's most respected pioneers. In the early years of gifted awareness, one of George Betts's colleagues had come to my small northeastern Colorado community recruiting gifted kids for his summer camp. I didn't piece this together until many years later when I attended one of George's sessions at the Colorado Association for Gifted and Talented state conference. As a part of that summer camp recruiting process, I took an IQ test. Although I took the test, my dad, a high school social studies teacher, was dubious. Parents didn't pay to send their kids to gifted camps in the 1970's—especially social studies teachers who held down extra jobs after school and on weekends at gas stations and auto parts stores to support their families.

My parents were told the results of the IQ test, but I'm not sure they ever shared them with me; even if they did, the numbers would have been meaningless to their son, who could recite many statistics from the backside of 1975 Topps baseball cards, and loved playing baseball even more. I assume that my IQ was somewhere between 50 and 150—somewhere between someone's second favorite teacher and someone's nineteenth favorite teacher.

In a lifetime as a teacher's kid and as a teacher—specifically working with gifted learners since 1997—I have learned above all that I love school and I love working with gifted kids. Of course there have been times when I would have taken any other job in the world to escape the frustration and aggravation. We have all felt those moments as teachers and as parents. Those challenging moments, however, were powerful in face of the joyful ones: the times we've fallen out of our desks laughing, the flashes of understanding or inspiration in a student's eyes, unexpected moments of sincere gratitude from a middle schooler, the hours and hours I've spent both worrying and smiling at the growth of so many kids—thousands of them—whose names I will suddenly remember when they reach out to me in their adult years. "You probably don't remember be, but..." "Oh, goodness! I do remember you. I really do."

People like to talk about the way teachers touch so many lives. I think of it just the opposite: I feel honored that I have been touched by the thousands of lives that have crossed my path in schools.

I hope you'll like what is in this book. I hope you will find yourselves nodding your head from time to time, relating to a story. I hope that several times you will see yourself, one of your children, or one of your students in the anecdotes. I hope you will not see this as a hard and fast collection of best practices. Instead, let's imagine we are having brown bag lunch together in the teacher's lounge, or a glass of wine in my back yard—a metaphorical holding of hands on the way to the bus without the kindergartner's karate chop. I'm pretty good at doing those things.

Chapter 1
A Place to Be Me

I Used to be Gifted previously appeared in the NAGC blog at NAGC.org.

I Used to Be Gifted

Next to me sits Matthew, a smoldering 4th grade boy. He's trying to keep all of the intensities inside, but they keep leaking out.

Impatience. He interrupts. His mom brings him back to the topic at the table—his advanced learning plan—but he is ready to launch into a detailed explanation of a tangent to a tangent to a thought he has connected.

Next to me, I can almost see his frequencies light up—the wires and electrons connecting, crossing, uncrossing, heading off and away at light speed. His mom keeps bringing him back. She knows him well. She's used to this.

We discuss Matthew's advanced learning plan and how things are going here in his new school. "Pretty good," he says, "…except for that brain thing."

"That brain thing?"

"I guess I might have a problem with my brain," he explains, looking at his mom for confirmation. She has heard about this already.

The "brain thing" comment has come from another boy in his class. Both his mother and I jump in with the same sort of comments and reassurances. This is the sort of mean thing others say to try to make you feel bad, and these people are trying to make you feel bad because they feel bad about themselves. Making you feel bad will make them feel better.

"I know," he says, but he is doubtful.

You have a problem with your brain. This is the sort of comment 4th grade boys throw around at one another. Instead of hurling rocks, they may hurl words—trying to tease, trying to get a rise out of others, seeing if someone will bite on the challenge. But Matthew has taken the comment to heart. Sitting next to me, I can see it. I can feel it. This comment hurts deeply. It's almost as if he is in mourning. His grief radiates.

Other boys would let the comment pass, maybe even laugh. Still others would fire back in some way, hurl an even bigger rock—try to even the score. Matthew's sensitivity, though, is profound. It is devastating. It is beautiful.

I fear the beauty will turn inward. It is so easily done.

One facet of the gifted brain appears to be not only a strong memory but also a strong association of memories with the feelings surrounding them. "Gifted children," Christine Fonseca states, "often will relive the feelings of significant moments in their lives, such as a move or the loss of a pet, over and over again."

Matthew will remember this.

◇◇◇

How many times has an adult said to me, "You teach gifted and talented? I used to be gifted…"

"Used to be?"

I have tried to explain to a gifted adult what they might be feeling. Maybe there was no such thing as a gifted and talented program when they were growing up. Maybe no one had ever talked to them about what being gifted was all about, or maybe when they had grown to a place in their lives where they were ready to accept their neurodiversity, there had been no community available to support such notions. Maybe life got in the way. Maybe they met with disapproval, were made to feel like an outsider. Maybe they felt like they had a *problem with their brain*. Maybe they stopped listening to their inside voice.

Yes, you were gifted. You still are. There is no *used to be* in any definition. Giftedness does not run out; it doesn't have a border; giftedness is a way of being. All your life you have been thinking things other people did not typically think about, making connections others did not easily make, *feeling* the world more intensely than others. To you, it just seemed normal…because the only head you truly lived freely in was your own.

And neuroscience shows that, yes, your brain is different from others. You do have a "brain thing," and it comes with challenges. Your neurologically divergent mind rapidly fires connections, deeply absorbs information, processes and reflects like a really "neato" flashing lights pinball machine—the coolest ones from the 1970s like the Elton John Pinball Wizard game. Amongst those many connections, you also carry an enormous capacity for compassion. You want actions to match words; you see hypocrisy and, come on, you can admit it (you are among friends here), you are sensitive and probably care about what others think a little bit too much.

"Oh?"

"Yes."

But all along, you were living your own personal poetry of the world…and unconsciously hiding that poetry inside yourself. Why did you learn to keep it muted, hidden? Did you fear that maybe you had a *brain thing*?

Is it those negative feelings that make you consider your giftedness as a thing of the past?

I wonder what it would take to make you feel safe enough to share that poetry inside yourself again.

References

Fonseca, Christine. 2016. *Emotional intensity in gifted students.* Waco TX: Prufrock Press.

Welcome Home

Outside my classroom in the first grade pod, I hear a ruckus. My colleague is escorting a squirming boy to a timeout in the hallway. His emotions have boiled over. Forehead scrunched into straight lines, his arms are a flurry as he whips around and sprints away from his teacher toward the kindergarten rooms around the corner.

His teacher and I make eye contact, and I nod. We've done this before. "I will keep an eye out for him," I tell her, as a visibly big sigh raises her shoulders up and down and she goes back inside her classroom full of 1st graders. We want to make sure this little boy is safe and doesn't flee the school building.

Except beyond me looking for him, he is watching out for me as I round the corner in the hallway. He too has done this before. He sprints ahead toward the school's foyer and the front doors. I quicken my pace so as not to lose sight of him. Instead of running to the doors, though, he dips into the open elevator, and the doors ding shut just as I arrive.

I walk past the elevator out into the foyer where I can see the top of the stairs and the elevator exit onto the 2nd floor from below. The elevator dings open. He peers out and sees me. Neither one of us moves for a moment—deciding what our next play will be. As I start up the stairs toward him, he sprints down the 5th grade hallway toward the back doors of the school. I can see the school psychologist upstairs walking down the third grade hallway on the opposite side to try to intercept him. I head back toward his classroom thinking that he may come down the back stairs, and I'm right.

I see the principal waiting outside his classroom door as I round the corner. Meanwhile, the school psychologist has come down the back stairs, and he is trapped. Frantically, he turns to dash back inside his classroom, but the door is locked.

"Let me in! Let me in!" He pounds on the door—flinging his body against it. Twisting the handle back and forth and pulling with all his might, he is desperate to go back to the place he has just run away from. This classroom, after all, is his home.

Who We Might Become

I am working the crosswalk after school, and another first grader skids to a stop in front of me—a real, actual, tennis-shoes-skidding-on-pavement-skid. Kids are always skidding to a stop. They don't just stop. Sometimes they skid to a stop and provide their own sound effects when they do it…*eeerrrrrch*!

This particular school year, I have come back from summer vacation with a goatee, having left clean shaven. The skidding first grader has come to a hard stop because something has suddenly dawned on him. He observes, "I used to know someone who looks like you."

"Oh?"

"His name was Mr. Hess, but he didn't have a beard."

"Well, that's me! I'm Mr. Hess. I grew a goatee," I say, rubbing my chin to emphasize the connection.

"Oh!" He's happy to learn this. Mystery solved! After a long pause, he says, "So what is your name now?"

I hadn't thought of that. I didn't know I got to pick a new name. I thought I could keep the old one. What an intriguing thought! Afterall, hadn't I just re-made myself?

Kids re-make themselves several times a day. On the playground, I see them mouthing words, talking to some imaginary character, waving sticks, fending off imaginary enemies as they bound across playground wood chips (bad idea, believe me, I'm a recess professional; nothing good can come from waving sticks on a playground). Let's get this straight: that bounding kid with the imaginary stick is not pretending to be Batman, he IS Batman.

Out of the blue, on a random day in March, for example, I will be asked, "Mr. Hess, who are you going to be for Halloween."

"Er…I don't know." I should know better as an elementary teacher that I ought to keep ready-made answers to these questions… like what is my favorite dinosaur, my favorite animal, my favorite planet, my favorite Power Puff Girl.

This question is not "what costume will I wear" or "how will I dress up" but WHO WILL I BE? It's not so much about Halloween as it is about hope, and that anything is possible when you are seven years old. And it makes me think…who will I be when October comes around? What will I have learned, how will I have grown, and how will these experiences have re-made me? Who WILL I be? Maybe I will just grow a goatee again.

"Brain development is asynchronous: throughout our lives, our brains have the ability to change…based on attention, intention, and experience" (Tetrault, p. 7). This is called 'neuroplasticity'. All people can change and grow, so much so that we may even need a new name. Ninety-eight per cent of our body's atoms are replaced over the course of 12 months (as reported in *This American Life*, episode 737, 5-14-2020). But some of our DNA, buried in cells of our hearts, brains, bones and teeth, stay with us our whole lives. On one level, we physically become almost a new person; but on another, we always remain who we are—the person we will always be in our hearts. The thought of this is both comforting and full of possibility and hope.

It is important to point out that we need the right environment to encourage growth, and that environment must include "emotional and social well-being and safety, and cultural well-bell being and 'belongingness'" (Miller and Clinkenbeard, p. 21). For gifted learners to grow to their potential, they need validation, affirmation, affiliation, and a feeling of affinity.

As a first grader myself, I adored my teacher Miss Snap. In her classroom, I always felt validated and affirmed—encouraged and safe to be me. I still remember the smell of my desktop as we put our heads down for a few minutes each day after recess. Miss Snap would switch off the lights and pull the big window shades down into a silent classroom. Sometimes she sang softly as she went about her preparations for the afternoon lessons while we closed our eyes and quietly breathed into our folded arms. Breathe, just breathe—our 1972 version of mindfulness. In my memory, Miss Snap's sweet voice swirled through the classroom and laid its quiet hands on my shoulders. These moments felt like home to me.

Think of the most wonderful teacher you've ever had. When this person comes to mind, I bet you can remember how you felt in their classroom. We might not remember the things that were said or specific things we did, but I'd wager we remember the way it all felt like home.

At Home in the Middle

Our culture has decided that it's OK to be gifted in certain ways, but somehow it is elitist to be intellectually gifted. If you can read an opposition's defense in football, check off at the scrimmage line to an alternative play, and then pass a football 50 yards between the cornerback and nickelback to a receiver running in full stride, you will be celebrated. (And by the way, that quarterback is most likely nonverbally gifted, and sees visual relationships better than 95% of the population). On the other hand, if you can pinpoint a metaphor in text at age 8 and infer the metaphor's relationship to the characterization of the protagonist, then this is somehow elitist. If your neighbors are investing in basketball camps and hockey gear and following their kids to tournaments, it may be wise for you not to mention that your child is in the gifted and talented program. As Delisle and Galbraith summarize, "Ours is an allegedly egalitarian nation. We're supposed to give all children the same opportunities to learn, grow, and realize their potential. We're not supposed to give some children special, better, extra opportunities. *That's not fair*" (p. 23). This concept of fairness is decidedly not democratic, specifically unfair to intellect as it prefers brawn over brain.

What if we spoke about intellectual giftedness in the same way we speak about gifted athletes? What if parents spoke about intellectual giftedness, posting photos and championship banners on social media, with the same sort of unabashed pride reserved for athletics?

"Did you hear about my daughter?"

"Yes! I saw your post. First team all-state literature analysis! Fantastic!"

◇◇◇

"Do you think you're special? Isn't everyone, after all, gifted?" Some districts have begun to declare everyone in need of more challenging opportunities. Appropriate challenge is always good, but failing to provide gifted programming fails to recognize the more specific needs of gifted students. I've heard gifted colleagues say that what is good for gifted students is good for all students. Taking that view, however, is minimalizing the needs of a neurologically diverse population. While I understand that we gifted professionals feel the need to include rather than exclude—that we, as gifted education professionals, must tread the line of perceived elitism—we must not contribute to the myth that gifted kids will be just fine on their own without interventions. We would never argue, for example, that all students should complete an accelerated math curriculum. Some districts, on the other hand, are eliminating gifted programming altogether—directly or indirectly declaring gifted programming elitist. In both scenarios, gifted kids lose.

And no, not everyone is gifted. All children are unique. All children's lives are precious. All children deserve love and support. But not all children are gifted. The brain of a gifted individual is biologically different; gifted learners are neurologically diverse. Neuroscience tells us that gifted learners have a larger brain volume, greater connectivity across brain regions, increased brain activation, greater sensory sensitivity, and increased brain areas associated with emotional processing (Sharon Duncan, et al.) This neurologically diverse individual will face many challenges and will likely encounter misunderstandings from friends, teachers, and colleagues throughout their lifetimes. Being gifted is not elitist. On the contrary, gifted individuals face potential for real struggle in this world as well as amazing creative and productive capacity.

One thing is certain, however: it's decidedly uncool to be gifted in middle school.

I had joked with my middle school's principal that if I were to teach gifted and talented and public speaking, my classroom would need to be in a portable space where we could do what we needed to do, be as noisy as we needed to be doing it, and not get on anyone else's nerves in the process.

Instead of our own building, she arranged for us to take residence in the former Home Economics room. Way up at the northwest corner of the school and far away from most of the action, windowless, avocado green metal cabinets, and with tile floors from 1970, that room was near perfect. Though the "Home Ec" room wasn't a separate building, it was a wonderful space for bright light shining out of lively eyes (or, almost as often, a kaleidoscope of unique focus in faraway looks), and the buzzing energy of gifted middle schoolers. While gifted kids experience life in layered intensities, middle school gifted kids experience life through some other adjective that often goes beyond the word *intensities*. Many days their emotions and hormones make them more akin to miniature Norse gods than middle schoolers…and I mean that comparison in all its passionate glory, both good and bad. We needed this huge classroom with tile floors so anyone could make their larger-than-life messes produced when gifted adolescent minds invoke Thor swinging his hammer and tossing around thunderbolts. Yes, I realize this is a quite a dramatic statement, but it beautifully characterizes the intensity of middle school.

The Home Economics room was full of quirky humor and inside jokes—those things families share that might only make sense at home. Why do gifted individuals so often find things humorous that others do not? "The gifted person with exceptionally greater connectivity across brain regions has more paths to follow, a potentially more rapid processing pace, and simply more unexpected turns available" (Duncan, et al, p. 3 in the section Greater Connectivity Across Brain Regions). Our classroom was inhabited by a pasta dragon, a stapler that talked, and a giant Snoopy Pez dispenser that coughed out full packages of Pez candy and took on its own personality. "Quiet! The Pez Speaks! You must respect the Pez!" We thought these things were hilarious. The unique power of this camaraderie didn't need the understanding of others for it to work for us.

I was guilty of encouraging this quirky humor. I started a classroom collection of creepy toys highlighted by a Furby whose fur could be removed (greatly enhancing its creepiness), and which would make random Furby cackling comments during class from inside a storage closet. Our collection included an alien baby, a robotic dog, and the King of Squirrels which lived safely tucked away in the back corner near the washer and dryer. If it was a toy and even a little bit creepy, someone brought it in. A foam head which used to display wigs from the old sewing room somehow became a prop in several students' presentations. Super Cup—a paper cup with pipe cleaner arms and wearing a construction paper leotard—flew over the classroom. Super Cup had been created in an open-ended assignment but had since attained legendary status with students over the years—some of whom were in kindergarten when Super Cup was created. On the first day of class, younger siblings of previous students would exclaim, "So there it is! My sister told me about Super Cup. Where's the Furby?"

One day, a 6th grader brought the Tickle Me Elmo she had gotten for Christmas when she was little—a toy that had been highly sought after half a decade earlier when the students were first graders. She turned it on and placed it on the floor, and as Elmo laughed and spun circles on the classroom floor, the students smiled and then began laughing. Then they began laughing harder, and as the synergy became more and more infectious, we couldn't stop laughing—even the couple of boys who were already too cool for gifted and talented classes. It didn't seem so out of the ordinary in the "Home Ec" room. The "Home Ec" room became a place where students wanted to be even when they weren't supposed to be there—like during lunch time. During 7th grade lunch (which was my lunch period as a teacher) there were anywhere from 2 to 12 kids hanging out in a steady rotation under the guise of practicing their public speaking events at any lunch period. During 6th and 8th grade lunches, students with passes could quietly enter with their lunch trays and go to my office to practice. The "quietly" rule was often broken, but shutting my office door against it actually only made the laughter from within even louder. Everyone needs a break, though, and some days I needed quiet time for myself and would declare the room off limits to all lunch periods.

Announcements, signs, and warnings like "No lunch group on Thursday. No appointments. No exceptions." sort of worked. At one faculty meeting, my principal smiled as she described one of these lunch-off-limits days. "I heard a commotion down at the far end of the hallway, and I turned the corner to find some of Mark's kids carrying their lunch trays and pounding on his classroom door. 'Let us in! Let us in!' As I got closer, I heard Mark hollering back from inside, 'Go away! Go away!'"

We understand that everyone needs a place that feels like home, and the neuroscience of learning supports the value of "strong interpersonal connections that respect each person's autonomy and individuality while linking him/her in empathic communication with others" (Malleability, plasticity, and individuality: How children learn and develop in context, p. 313). Positive relationships have an affect size of 0.74 for learning—a truly monster affect size in educational research terms (Sapolsky, 2007, as shared by Erick Jensen, 7-27-2018, Colorado State Gifted Symposium). In short, where and with whom can one just be oneself in a safe and accepting atmosphere ideal for learning? There may be no other time more important in a gifted child's life than in middle school.

It is a myth that most gifted kids do not do well socially. A culture which often chooses to view giftedness as elitism, or embraces anti-intellectualism, uses the "misfit nerd" stereotype as a hard poke in the ribs. In numerous studies, however, gifted children are shown to be more highly regarded in prosocial behaviors such as sociability, leadership, cooperation, and friendliness. This is true, however, only until middle school. "Gifted adolescents are attuned to the social disadvantages of being labeled *gifted* and identify social consequences as being the worst thing about being gifted" (Peairs, Putallaz, and Costanzo, p. 186).

Gifted boys came to the "Home Ec" room full of wonderful ideas and quirky interests; but many times through 7th and 8th grade began to be too cool for giftedness. A gifted girl's confidence is at its highest at age 10—at which point her confidence sinks lower and lower until it finally begins to rebound later in the college years. Her self-confidence will not return to 4th grade levels until she is 50 (Cline and Short). Over the years, gifted girls came into my 6th grade classroom with a beautiful shining light in their eyes—leaders, confident in their viewpoints, and expressive. By eighth grade, many of them had become quieter and quieter and quiet. One of these now quiet girls, Jennifer, expressed her secret solace in high achievement at the end of 8th grade like this: "I believe that if I get a good grade on a test that everything will be fine, and if I don't let anything bother me or if I act good, then my life will be good. I believe that these things I do will help my life, and it's the only thing that feels as if I'm doing something to help patch the hole in my heart." The "Home Ec" room was the place where these words could be written honestly—a place for "empathic communication with others." For some, it was even a place to help patch a hole in a heart.

I am always a bit on guard when I read parenting advice. Who is to say one parent's experience and viewpoint will fit my parenting world? Who is to say my teacher's advice is the key to unlock some sort of secret wonderfulness? I can confidently say, though, that everyone needs a place to feel safe and connected, to be one's true self, or as one middle schooler put it in a thank you card when she graduated from high school, a place to be "inspired to be strange." "As guides," Nicole Tetrault states, "we need to allow space and time for the bright mind to break free from the ordinary, experience the extraordinary, and then awaken to life" (p. 25).

I want to make sure I am not painting too ideal of a picture. Of course not everyone saw the "Home Ec" room as home. We all process our experiences in different ways. Once upon a time when I was having a "see me after class" chat with a boy who was struggling with behavior issues, I said, "Shawn, we have 100 more days, one hour a day, to figure out how we are going to make this work."

"Unfortunately," was his reply.

Teaching middle school is full of humbling experiences.

One's True Self

Who are you, and what does gifted really mean anyway? You are excitable and intense. You quickly make mental connections and are apt to bound into metaphors. You feel things deeply. You are receptive, sensitive and open, even when you are trying not to be. You are curious, imaginative and creative about so many things, yet driven to find out more and more, and even more about particular and sometimes obscure or slightly oddball topics. You can do so many things, yet that definitely doesn't mean you are good at everything. You are independent and feel connections with others, no matter their age, who experience the world in similar ways. When you are eight years old and in a small group discussion and you mention that you have been wondering about death: What happens when you die? Does your mind go on thinking, and are you still you without your body when you die? This is a time when you need other kids around you who nod their heads because they get it: existential thinking at age eight. They've thought about these sorts of things, too. Yes, you are OK. They are kindred spirits. This place—these people—they feel right to you.

In establishing a healthy identity, Andrew Mahoney cites four psychological constructs which gifted learners undergo. The first is validation, which is a recognition that one's gifts exist as confirmed by others—what most often happens through the gifted identification process. The second construct is affirmation. One's identity as a gifted learner is affirmed through repeated interactions with parents or teachers or other students, for example. A common affirmation in education occurs through participation in a gifted program. For many students, this affirmation may be haphazard or may never come at all—depending on a school's commitment to services and resources.

The third construct is affiliation, where one associates with others who share "similar intensities, passions, desires and abilities" (p 6). When I think about affiliation, I think of the social media group for gifted adults in which several posts a week start with something similar to "I know people will understand where I'm coming from in this group, so I feel safe in posting this… " or "This group seems like the right place to ask this question. Do you ever experience (insert quirky behavior) like I do?" As with the gifted adults group, gifted classrooms, pullout groups, certain clubs, Saturday enrichment classes, and other places gifted kids gather encourage a togetherness, and promote an understanding of oneself and one's orientations and tendencies through affiliation with others who are similar. As Mahoney concludes, "Affiliating the gifted aspects of self is conceivably one of the strongest methods to relieve the alienation and isolation that gifted people so often feel" (p. 6).

The fourth construct is affinity, which Mahoney describes as a transcendent and soulful quality of identity and connectedness where one's self becomes connected to the larger world. Affinity, through its synergy, relieves "the existential angst associated with being gifted" (p.7). A gifted fourth grader who had achieved a sense of affinity gave me the best gift I've ever received during teacher appreciation week—a thank you note that said, "You cut the lines between weird and unique. Unique wins. Thank you for helping me realize it's not weird, but unique." Affinity is also what I call "home."

6th grader Emily came to the gifted program having been identified based on her nonverbal ability score in the 95th percentile. As the scoring guide for the Cognitive Ability Test explains, "Students who show a relative strength on the Nonverbal Battery can be either very good at reasoning with spatial stimuli or particularly adept at solving novel problems that are unlike those encountered at school." Emily's nonverbal score goes far beyond a "relative strength." Her verbal and quantitative scores are somewhere around the 50th percentile. On paper, she may identify as twice-exceptional, but that label doesn't get her any support without identifying her individual strengths and needs. All of her data points add up to a challenge to the school system, but most importantly, these data points are not just a set of scores: They represent an individual who is unique and precious and still full of hope in 6th grade.

As a champion for kids with nonverbal strengths who are not built for school, I was eager to see how Emily's individual giftedness might shine in a classroom full of gifted kids, full of alternative assignment menus, and full of independent projects to meet academic standards. If giftedness could be expressed in a sweet disposition, an infectious laugh, and the size of a smile, it would have been transparent from day one where Emily's strengths lay. It was not that simple, however, and even on the watch for her brilliance in my classroom, it took over a year for me to see it.

With the first written work it quickly became evident that her nonverbal gifts would not be expressed in reading or writing. "Not surprising," I thought. "I bet she's artistic!"

Nope.

"Hmmm...she will probably do well with STEM opportunities."

Another no. A craft saw and hot glue nightmare, her designs fell apart while Emily smiled through her attempts.

She made friends easily, seemed to get along with everyone no matter who they were. Could we call those qualities her gift?

Maybe. But there must be something more I was not seeing.

I'm not sure I saw even a flash of brilliance (except that brilliant smile) all the way through 6th grade—even with the myriad product choices offered on assignments.

Literature analysis? Um…a definite no.

Science? Not really.

Math? Still no.

In the "Home Ec" room, many of the gifted students were also enthusiastic participants on the speech team I coached. The forensics/speech team was another way to celebrate our glorious geekiness not just with each other, but also in affiliation with other gifted kids in our geographic region. Because the "Home Ec" room was also the gifted and talented room and the forensics room, each Friday I offered students the opportunity to replace the day's activities with a performance of a forensics event they'd like to try. Emily chose creative storytelling one morning—an event in which the participant is given a character, a setting and a situation, and has 30 minutes to prepare a 3-to-6-minute presentation in which they improvise their original story using only one notecard as a memory aid.

Emily emerged from my office 30 minutes later with her notecard in hand and proceeded to act out her story for our class. Her performance was far more than just good. A couple of her classmates literally fell out of their desks laughing. There it was! Her brilliance had shone! Students strong in nonverbal ability often can interpret others' postures, facial expressions, gestures, movements, and tones of voice in deeper communicative nuances than others. This ability to "read" others sometimes helps make them strong leaders, reliable listeners, and good friends. Emily has used this strength to create, mimic, and act out humorous scenarios in creative storytelling.

A gifted kid is a gifted kid is a gifted kid is a gifted kid…even when she doesn't fit in school. Even when she may need a safe place to exhibit her gifts. Even when it may take more than a year to have the right opportunity to show it.

Yet the detractors will insist she's intelligent but not very practical. Sure he's smart, but he's not very good in social situations. She's brilliant but so scattered. Gifted maybe…but not well behaved. How many times have you heard these things? They are our culture's passive-aggressive attempts to knock intellectual giftedness down to size. Do we say, "Sure, she has a beautiful singing voice…but she can't figure out the corporate tax code."? Do we say, "He has qualified for the Olympic Games, but he's not very skilled at laying hardwood floors."? Next time you hear "school smart, sure, but not street smart," try replying "a state champion in the 1500 meter run, sure, but doesn't speak fluent French."

◇◇◇

Another 6th grade boy identified gifted because of his nonverbal ability—another school year. This boy has discovered that his chair makes a vibrating noise if he pushes it—just so—across the linoleum. In my mind, he is Lawnmower Boy—the quirkiest of all superheroes.

"I'm mowing the lawn." Other students smile.

He is deeply amused by this vibrating quirk of physics, and mowing the lawn is repeated morning after morning until it becomes a welcome ritual in our classroom.

Lawnmower Boy hates to write. His handwriting is that of a student much younger—blocky print of different sizes. He grudgingly writes responses to literature in a notebook that is falling apart. His written words move diagonally across the page, and he ignores the lines altogether.

He volunteers to read one of his literature responses aloud during a class discussion, and his humorous interpretation draws laughter. The next response he writes is longer, and I notice him giggling to himself as he writes it. This response draws more laughter when he reads it. He begins to write much longer responses—off-the-wall humor somehow that still relates appropriately (most of the time, anyway) to the subject matter in the classroom. Later in the year, he is not just reading the responses but regularly performing them. Outside of the "Home Ec" room, he drives his language arts teacher crazy. In language arts class, he hardly writes anything at all. He loses focus and can be disruptive. But in 7th grade science class, the teacher has struck a deal. If this boy stays mostly on task throughout the week on science assignments, then he can have the last 15 minutes on Friday to perform for the class. The science teacher gets it—has two gifted kids of his own. Our boy makes good on the deal every week.

At the end of 7th grade, we make our own deal in the "Home Ec" room. Well, it's not so much a deal as reaching an understanding: "You are driving your language arts teacher insane," I tell him.

He nods quietly and apologetically. He's a good kid. He already knows this.

"She is a nice person. She wants to see you doing well. So how about it?"

We had built a relationship and an understanding. He was in a place one hour each day where classmates appreciated his talent. He had a home, and he seemed amenable.

Each spring after exhausting state testing, our district followed with yet another achievement test to check on district growth standards. Some of my gifted students found this pointless. Their scores on these additional tests actually appeared as if they had regressed. This was not going to impress any administrator, and no gifted class should exist to raise test scores. I understand, however, that social-emotional growth, the opportunity to express one's individuality, and the affinity generated by the best gifted programming cannot ever take place if there is no 'home' where it might occur. That's why I began opening our late year testing sessions with this disclaimer: "I know everyone is tired of taking tests, but would you please just try hard for the next 30 minutes? Some people are scoring lower than in September, and it makes it look like this class is a waste of time. If that keeps happening, someone is eventually going to want to get rid of this class altogether." The scores soared. Even middle school gifted kids didn't want to lose their home.

That spring, to his English teacher's astonishment, Lawnmower Boy scored at the advanced level on both reading and writing on the state assessments.

"I did it because she promised a candy bar to anyone who could score advanced," he told me, but I knew that is only just a little bit true.

Do you have students who avoid reading and writing? Here is a free menu of independent reading projects to help them along. https://www.teacherspayteachers.com/Product/Menu-of-Independent-Reading-Projects-FREE-Enrichment-and-GATE-4166108

Studio Time

On a sunny Friday in the spring, a huddle of five gifted fourth graders has erupted in laughter. One student sits at a computer while four others look over her shoulder, sometimes pointing at the monitor and commenting. They have skipped "extra" Friday recess to be here.

We called it "studio time." Having the rare luxury in this profession of teaching full-time as a gifted resource teacher in one elementary school, I reserved Friday afternoons for studio time—up to two and a half hours to work on any project of one's choosing. Students could request studio time in half hour increments with signed permission forms from their classroom teachers. One teacher who was particularly supportive would allow his gifted students to come to studio time for the entire afternoon. Studio time was active and loud and deathly to my materials and supplies budget, but it may have been the most important opportunity we offered for gifted programming during the week.

Gifted students are often not well suited to working in groups, but during studio time these same students spontaneously formed groups with other kids just like them—often because a project one student was creating was so wonderful that others wanted to be in on it. One of the social-emotional lessons we were learning was that "copying" is one of the greatest compliments a creative person could receive, and as generous classmates, the most creative students brought others on board with their enthusiasm. The unique formation of working teams always required conflict and negotiation skills. From time to time there were hurt feelings, and many times enthusiastic responses didn't meet the vision and direction of leadership. Groups formed and unformed like classic rock and roll bands within one afternoon with splinter groups sometimes creating parallel and competing projects. I tried to stay out of it. It was interesting to watch it all unfold—an open but guided "growing up" process right in front of me. Many projects became grand. Many projects died from one Friday to the next.

We didn't have enough space to store all of the projects in my classroom. We had to come up with rules about how long both finished and unfinished projects could take up shelf space. I don't know how many times I tripped over projects on the floor, and we had our own yellow caution tape to attempt to keep this from happening. One time when I encouraged a student to take home his project because it was nearing the "throw away" deadline, he simply dumped it into the trash. "Mom said my room is already too full. I'm not allowed to keep new projects unless I throw away an old one first." The pain of parenting gifted children, huh? Many projects were abandoned (the parts salvaged and returned to the craft bins), and this was OK, too—a key part of the creative process.

Sometimes the room was very quiet, students engaged and concentrating without the need for any words; but typically it was buzzing. I heard conversations between students about sharing passions, about what was fair or unfair, about world events that worried them, as well as many enthusiastic conversations about quirky hobbies and interests. All of a sudden, I would have a classroom full of pangolin enthusiasts, dragon novel groupies, or flags of the world experts. Teams of miniature skate park builders raced through the doorway. "We want to be able to skate at night. Do you have Christmas lights and batteries?" I didn't, but the next week we did! Suddenly it would become extremely important to read all of the books in the *Warriors* cat adventure series. And why is your class library, Mr. Hess, missing some of the books in the series? Apparently, it might seem, I was out to ruin their lives by not having all of the dozens of *Warriors* books available in sequence. And by the way, which *Warriors* cat clan would I be a part of if I were a cat (it turns out I would be a proud member of Water Clan)? A team of 5th grade girls decided they would stage a trash bag fashion show. The trash bag fashion show eventually evolved into a carnival they would host for 3rd graders with homemade games and real prizes. On their own, the group was more active than the school's student council. Somehow, the evolution from trash bag fashion show to carnival was a perfectly logical unfolding of events.

One third grade boy came every week to share with me a backpack full of his creations and collections, including coins from all over the world and some replicas he'd made himself from cardboard. At home, he was building three-dimensional models of famous buildings. When Notre Dame burned, he was devastated. Inside my classroom he worked on projects only sporadically. He just wanted to be there—quietly and pleasantly observing the other students after he shared his newest creation or collection with me. He would hold his backpack in front of him, stealthily snake his hand down inside, and then present each item to me. "Do you know what I have inside here?" he would ask in his quiet way—every single time. I often had to lean very close to hear him.

"I don't know. A baby chinchilla?" I would venture.

"No," he would smile but answer very sincerely. "This is the Poland Country Ball." He was keenly interested in anything that had to do with geography and had begun creating what he called "country balls"—paper balls, their size based on the land area of various countries, that were decorated with symbols particular to each country they represented. Where else would we see such a thing but down in the studio? Next, he produced his drawing of a 5 Euro note—detailed and impressively accurate—as well as the cardboard cut-outs of his version of coins from around the globe.

This was the same boy who told the speech therapist that his first language was Swedish. His teacher, upon learning this, was embarrassed to have referred him for speech services. Why wouldn't his mother have mentioned such a thing? Why? Because it wasn't true. Like many who attended studio time, he didn't fit very well in his classroom upstairs even though he had a very supportive teacher. These wonderful and quirky personalities made teaching gifted kids such a challenge at times, but mostly such a joy.

In a string of construction projects, 4th grader Noah has drilled tiny holes in craft sticks and has inserted wooden pegs cut from a dowel as joints to create a miniature, extendable wooden "arm." He wonders if he can make "fingers" that will pick items up as well. He comes to studio time every Friday with a desperate look on his face, whirls about the room, and simply needs to "build something." In one quarter he has built a glider made from dowels and trash bags, a foosball table from a cardboard box and wooden clothespins, and an aircar driven with a grocery bag for a sail, amongst other things. Upstairs in his classroom, he is not doing so well academically or socially.

As a boy who likes to build stuff, he doesn't fit an elementary school system that predominantly relies on developing reading and writing skills. His classroom teacher sometimes requires him to complete a missing assignment in order to be allowed to attend studio time—which he does. This is a requirement I support, by the way, because his teacher is understanding and supportive of gifted kids, and because both of us are trying to help him understand about the importance of sometimes "doing things you don't always like to do" because they build essential academic skills. He is not bored by the curriculum. Sadly, his skill set simply does not fit. He wants to build stuff—not write stuff. We see his potential to fall into an underachievement cycle later in middle school and high school. Can we intercept that potential in 4th grade while he has the support of teachers who understand him?

So many gifted kids over the years just didn't quite fit the system. I have always said that the luckiest kid in the school, academically, has scored in the 50th percentile on all ability tests. This student is the luckiest because the school system is built to challenge this student appropriately each and every day. Many gifted kids over the years have achieved wonderfully as well. They've been leaders, kind to others, and active, high achievers who win citizenship awards, athletes and actors and artists and performers of all sorts. Neurological diversity is exactly that—diverse. The check mark in the box on student records beside "identified gifted" indicates a need to try to understand this student and to provide services which help this student thrive. There should be an asterisk there as well, and noted at the bottom of the page should be "Make sure to help this student find others like themselves where their identities are confirmed—a place that feels like home."

Here is a free tool for reluctant writers like Noah: https://www.teacherspayteachers.com/Product/One-Page-Non-fiction-Response-for-Reluctant-Writers-3rd-8th-2473864

Coming Home

I think my son was about five years old when he hit the most famous of home runs out in the yard. I was pitching a plastic baseball to him, and he swung a big orange plastic bat, hitting a soft grounder directly to me.

He looked at me. I looked at him…and then he took off toward the piece of wood that marked first base.

"I'm going to get you!" I reached to tag him but, oh-so-close, I missed, and he was safe at first. He stood there giggling at me as I turned around and walked back to my position at pitcher.

I was fairly sure that I knew how it would go from here. When I heard laughter behind me as he took off running toward second, my suspicions were confirmed.

"Hey!" I shouted, holding that ball out straight in the I'm-going-to-tag-you-and-you-can't-get-away-from-me gesture. "You better not try to steal a base on me!"

I just somehow oh-so-barely missed the tag again. As he stood safe at second base, I told him that he better not even think about running to third when I turned around. Then I promptly turned around so that his laughter flew off toward third base, and of course, I just (oh-so-close) missed tagging him out as he and I laughed all the way past short stop.

At third, he didn't even bother waiting until I turned around or warned him before he ran toward home. I chased behind, now laughing as hard as my son.

Have you ever laughed so hard that you couldn't catch your breath? Have you ever laughed so hard that you cry in joy and can't figure out where the laughing ends and the crying begins? Have you ever laughed so hard that you lose the ability to stand upright?

Neither of us actually made it to home plate that day. We fell down in the yard on the baseline, unable to catch our breath. Neither of us had made it to home plate, but we had both made it home.

Gifted kids are bound to crash and fall from time to time just like all of us do. It is very important for them to remember, though, that somewhere out there is the right place at the right time with the right people who know and understand.

I hope someday you find this home, yourself, if you have not—that those you love in your family and in your classroom find this home each day they are with you. I hope that you always have a home to run back to and that the door is unlocked and wide open when you get there. I hope that you find a place and people to be with who fully accept your true and imperfect self. I hope that someday you laugh so hard running the bases that you joyously collapse, laughing, onto home plate.

References

Cantor, Pamela. Osher, David. Berg, Juliette, Steyer, Lily. Rose, Todd. 2019. Malleability, plasticity, and individuality: How children learn and develop in context. Applied Developmental Science, 23:4, 307-337.

Delisle, Jim. Galbraith, Judy. 2002. *When gifted kids don't have all the answers.* Free Spirit.

Duncan, Sharon. Goodwin, Corin. Haase, Joanna. Wilson, Sarah. Accessed June 2021. Neuroscience of giftedness. *Gifted Research and Outreach.* www.gro-gifted.org/the-neuroscience-of-giftedness/

Mahoney, Andrew. In search of the gifted identity: From abstract concept to workable counseling constructs. Accessed online July, 2021. Counseling the Gifted. www.counselingthegifted.com

Miller, Erin M. Clinkenbeard, Pamela R. 2021. Find the signal and ignoring the noise. *Parenting for High Potential.* National Association for Gifted Children. Vol 10. Issue 2.

Peairs. Putallaz. Costanzo. 2019. From a (aggression) to v (victimization): Peer status and adjustment among academically gifted students in early adolescence. *Gifted Child Quarterly*, 63:3

Tetrault, Nicole. 2020. *Insight into a bright mind.* Goshen, KY: Gifted Unlimited LLC.

Chapter 2
It's Who We Are

A previous version of *Could You Please Just Act Normal?* was Published in the SENG Library at sengifted.org.

Flourish. Enter a Gifted Kid.

Sometimes we forget to remember the wonderful qualities and delightful intensities our gifted children offer. As parents and therapists and educators, we are deeply concerned about the well-being of our gifted children. Perhaps that's why we tend to think of the social-emotional aspects of giftedness as issues to be addressed, problems to overcome, or roadblocks to thriving. As Dr. Linda Silverman states, after all, "Asynchronicity is certainly not a source of envy" (The Construct of Asynchronous Development, p. 37). But let's stop for a moment in all our worrying and concern and reflect on the delight our gifted children bring to our lives. In moments of frustration, we might forget the essential asynchronicity of giftedness is also a source of beauty.

I first taught gifted learners on the ground floor of the 1923 wing of Manitou Springs Elementary. Eight feet tall windows looked out onto a parking lot to the west, but if you stepped up close and looked between the trees and houses in the neighborhood, you could see Pikes Peak. My classroom floor was the original hardwood—layers of clear finish with symmetrical patterns of dots from where the desks had been bolted in place once upon a time. A slate blackboard spanned the wall behind my big oak desk. On it, a teacher's name was etched in an elegant cursive script. Apparently, the teacher had used something sharp to write her name, and there it was, looking over my shoulder almost 80 years later.

Upstairs, Intensities were Brewing

At that time, much of our gifted programming relied upon pull-out talent pool groups, and stacked above my room on the second and third floors were the third and fifth grade classrooms. At their appointed times each day, I would hear thumps and scrambling noises from the classrooms above—scurrying and scratching like mice in the ceiling. I imagined one of them to be a gifted student in my group, realizing it was time to come to my room, casting aside a textbook and slamming shut their desktop, already fast-walking toward the classroom door with arms and legs swinging stiffly and quickly—a gait students reserve for fast movement that won't get them in trouble for running. Classmates also in my talent pool group, seeing they were about to be left behind, rushed to follow the lead and "stiff-quicked" it to the door, too. Then followed the sound of feet on the stairs: clitter-claps of quick steps echoing, leaping and bounding thumps, jackets rustling and swishing around the stairwell corner a half flight up. Excited chatter almost always brought the words of one kid running behind others admonishing those running in front that they shouldn't be running. "Stop running!" was responded to with "I'm not running; you're the one who's running!" I always thought this was funny, and it's one more reason I'm not always reliable at recess duty.

Then—most suddenly—the first kid would appear in my classroom doorway.

If I got to write the script for the movie that will never be filmed of the rush down the stairs and the appearance of a gifted kid in my doorway, I would use Shakespeare's stage direction of *Flourish. Enter the king*. As an undergraduate English major, I had to look up the meaning of *flourish*. Dummies.com instructs us that Shakespeare meant *flourish* as fanfare and trumpets usually accompanying the entrance or exit of a king. *Flourish* is a perfect fit for the gifted kid's entrance. Students don't simply walk into our gifted and talented classrooms; they leap and run and gallop and, one time most memorably, cartwheel. They appear in the doorway almost like the stereotypical whoosh of a stage magician's cape: "ta da!" And yes, I know there is no running allowed in a hallway, and definitely no leaping downstairs. I know that flourishes—even smiling ones—may be disruptive. And yes, you are running even though you're "stiff-quicking" it. A school system built upon straight lines is not built for kids who want to create brilliance in dazzling swirls.

The excitement—this flourish—comes from the physical, intellectual, and emotional intensities of gifted learners. Its source comes from a teacher allowing gifted kids to get away with running. No, not running down the stairs...but running with challenges and creativity and projects and opportunity to explore passions. These kids just have to know. They have to create. They are impelled to discover. They must express themselves. No, not later...but now! They need runways.

Upstairs in their classroom—despite excellent classroom teachers often overwhelmed with the myriad of needs to be met—the kids who enter with a flourish are not flourishing in the other definition of the word. They spend one-fourth to one-half of their time waiting for others to catch up (*Misdiagnosis and Dual Diagnosis of Gifted Children*, online). They come to school each year with no need to review up to 24 to 70% of the curriculum they've already mastered (White Paper on Curriculum Compacting). Please understand this is not written to denigrate my colleagues working in the regular classroom. They are the hardest working people I know—doing so much for so many with so very little. As Jim Delisle states in "Differentiation Doesn't Work," our classroom teachers, despite their best efforts, often do not have the resources, the time, or the opportunity to meet the needs and intensities of their gifted students. This is why the groups who come bounding into my class can't wait to get to the room where the desks are no longer bolted to the floor.

Here lies the beauty in their energy and in their passion for learning. Ta-daaaa! Here I am! Let's get crackin' already! Our kids are looking for curriculum, as recommended in *Living with Intensity,* that encourages "original thought that develops intellectual risk-taking, and that requires full engagement of the intellect, world view, social/emotional aspects, and moral reasoning" (p. 71).

Two big cabinets filled with craft supplies and tools stood against the south wall of our classroom. The hot glue station lined the front of the room. The shelves under the big windows held craft saws, boxes of craft sticks, dowels, and wood scraps. Piles of cardboard—stacked neatly at the beginning of class—regularly ended up in disarray and were in constant need of tidying. Someone might accuse us of having fun, and they would absolutely be right…partially. This fun, contrary to what some might imagine, is wrapped in standards one to three grade levels ahead. The challenges come hands-on, are tied to real life experiences, involve choice and self-expression, and are evaluated with rubrics bent on processes and possibilities, not grades. In more than two decades of working with gifted kids, only once or twice has a student asked if they would get a grade for what they were doing. They're learning, after all, not simply *going to school.* There is a difference.

All of the best educators I've met over the years—and I have been blessed to meet so many—understand this difference.

The combination of advanced cognitive abilities and heightened intensity, the Columbus Group (1991) states, "create inner experiences and awareness that are qualitatively different from the norm." Often what is good for gifted kids is not good for all kids, and vice-versa. Everyone should have the opportunity to learn at appropriately challenging levels, but those levels must often be fast, deep, and rich to meet the intensities of gifted learners. The same kid who won't complete an assignment because they already knew all about it and is bored is the same kid who runs down the stairs to work on an independent project. The same kid who questions the justice of classroom rules is the same kid who leads a school initiative to collect winter clothing donations. The same kid who drives parents crazy because she never stops asking why, how, and how come is the same kid who, at age 12, develops a device that could send water quality information via Bluetooth (see the Gitanjali Rao bio online). I used to buy 500-count boxes of mini hot glue sticks and 1000-count boxes of craft sticks and make dozens of box-cutter blades dull while cutting stacks of cardboard in various sizes to be used for projects. I didn't bother with a check-out process for my classroom library because often novels were read and returned the next day anyway, and really, if that book is so important to you that you'll never return it, then fine…you should keep it.

Crying because she witnessed a tree being chopped down. Asking for a baby velociraptor for Christmas. Donating their young life's savings to the Red Cross. Building a catapult from 2 x 4s and garage doors springs that would throw a basketball across the parking lot. Skipping recess to work on a marble maze that would be hidden inside a pyramid. Giftedness can be a beautiful mess.

Flourish. Enter a gifted kid.

References

Curriculum Compacting. Accessed 2021. NAGC Online https://www.nagc.org/resources-publications/gifted-education-practices/curriculum-compacting

Daniels, Susan, and Piechowski, Michael M. Eds. *Living with Intensity*. Great Potential Press: 2009.

Delisle, Jim. 2015. Differentiation Doesn't Work. *Education Week*. Accessed Online https://www.edweek.org/teaching-learning/opinion-differentiation-doesnt-work/2015/01

Silverman, Linda Kreger. "The Construct of Asynchronous Development." *Peabody Journal of Education* Number 72, Vol 3-4. Lawrence Erlbaum Associates, Inc: 1997.

Webb, James T. Amend, Edward R. Amend. Webb, Nadia E. Goerss, Jean. Beljan, Paul, and & F. Olenchak, F. Richard. 2011. *Misdiagnosis and Dual Diagnosis of Gifted Children*. SENG Library Online https://www.sengifted.org/post/misdiagnosis-and-dual-diagnosis-of-gifted-children

The Exhilaration of Effortless Running

As adults, it may be difficult to remember the feeling of effortless running that we had as children. Every year our joints have gotten a little more creaky. We begin to understand our parents (you know, those really old people?) talking about being stiff from "sleeping wrong". We wake up with an injured knee, contemplate dry needling. How did I injure my knee just sleeping? We never used to read reviews to make sure we buy the right shoes and to make sure we employ the right stretching routines before going on a run. As kids, we just ran no matter what shoes we were wearing, no matter the weather, no matter if it was up hill, downhill, over rocks, or through mud—no need for stretching or yoga. We don't run that way anymore. Maybe we have gotten hurt somewhere along the way. We have felt too many disappointments, perhaps. Too many times we have fallen, and each time it has gotten a little more difficult to get back up again. Maybe we've made the decision that it's safer to walk—safer, maybe, not to even try a little smooth gliding over even ground. Maybe we started listening to those who told us to slow down. "What's your hurry, anyway?" Maybe we started saying that we used to be gifted.

One of my favorite descriptions of gifted children will always be Stephanie Tolan's *Is it a Cheetah?*: "Other cats retract their claws to keep them sharp, like carving knives kept in a sheath —the cheetah's claws are designed not for cutting but for traction. This is an animal biologically designed to run."

Effortless running, that kind of running we all experienced as the recess doors opened, is a release—a letting go of this world and a brief glimpse at the beauty in perfection. All children know how to do it—gifted children especially. Gifted children are cheetahs. They run faster and faster and sometimes even fly. It's an instinct, a reaction. Gifted kids are built for speed.

Could You Please Just Act Normal?

Once there was a highly gifted girl who ran through my classroom almost every day.

It's parent-teacher conference day. Ava, Lucy, and Emma—three sisters all in my gifted and talented groups—sweep into my room ahead of their parents. Eyes aglow, they wear huge smiles from the glowing reports they've received upstairs in their regular classrooms.

At the conference desk, Ava and Emma are eager to share their gifted and talented advanced learning plans and the projects they've undertaken. They lean in, their antennas up, their eyes sweeping back and forth between their parents and me. Lucy, however, is on the move. She has taken out her multi-tiered cardboard mini-golf project and has set it up on a table. She dashes across the room and back to retrieve craft sticks and tools. Needing another item, she hip-slides across a table (I'm serious, she really did this!), gallops to the supply area, and then returns to her project by ducking under that same table she has just slid across. She, too, is listening to the conversation and is eager to share—pausing ever-so-quickly to nod or add a comment. While her sisters wear expectant expressions, Lucy always seems to be on the verge of *doing* something, of going somewhere, of vaulting into action. Saying so, however, would be an understatement. The fact is that Lucy always IS doing something, going somewhere, or vaulting into action—not on the verge of it.

We all pause for a moment in our conversation to regard Lucy. "We cut out her naps by age 3 because if she napped for even 10 minutes in the car, she would be up until midnight," her mother tells me. "She has always had more energy than her sisters. She cannot sit still for very long even when she is engaged in her favorite pastime of reading. She frequently reads lying on her back, feet in the air moving like she is pedaling a bicycle."

As she crosses in front of us; we all turn to look at Lucy and smile as she smiles back at us.

Lucy's sisters Ava and Emma, myself, and most of the kids who are in my gifted and talented program live in the world of 95's—95th percentiles in ability, that is. As Susan Daniels and Elizabeth Meckstroth describe it in *Living with Intensity* (Daniels and Piechowski, 2009, p. 35), our lives as 95s are rich with intensities and overexcitabilities. Our minds receive, process, and filter frequencies from 240 cable channels in HD, while the typical person gets basic cable—maybe 35 stations. Lucy, however, is highly gifted. Her ability profile scores read 99s across the board. She began reading before kindergarten—a grade she skipped, by the way. Patricia Gatto-Walden once stated in her session at the Colorado Association for Gifted and Talented state conference, that the exceptionally and profoundly gifted may receive 5,000 or 10,000 channels and frequencies. Sure, we 95s may be apt to race passionately from one topic to the next, may be prone to rapid, staccato diatribes on different topics, may feel empathy deeper than others and be ready to save the world…but when it comes down to it, we can usually blend in pretty well with everyone else. Not true for 99+s. 95s are bubbling and usually running…but 99+s radiate and never stop running. They sizzle. They glow. They burst.

It has taken me a long time to properly process the wisdom of *Living with Intensity*. I've lived a lifetime in the world of 95s—in my own intensities—and because 95 is my reality and I usually blend in pretty easily, I've never really felt any different from anyone else. The behaviors of most of my students seem perfectly normal to me. I have to chuckle from time to time when someone dear to me points out one of my intensities. What? Everyone is not like that? I've started to watch my highly gifted kids more closely, though—my twice-exceptional kids as well—and I have begun to see more clearly their deeper intensities and recognize their behaviors not as deviant or baffling…but normal, yes normal *for them*.

So here is Lucy again…and you better look quickly…because there she goes, running across my classroom…normal. I don't think I've ever seen her walk from place to place. Normal.

We have craft saws and hot glue and long, poky dowel sticks in my classroom. Running is simply not safe.

"Lucy, what are you doing?" I ask her.

"Running?" she says, a question in her voice, and this said, of course, while she is running. It's normal.

"What are you supposed to be doing?" I ask her.

Still running, she turns very briefly in my direction, "Walking and being safe?"

"Can you do that?" I ask, her eyes gleaming a wonderful intensity. Normal.

"Yes?" she asks, maybe trying to convince herself, still running… and I know things are normal in my classroom, normally happening the way they should be according to the particular intensities of the unique, normal energy in a body and mind normally set to 5,000 frequencies, normal overexcitabilities, and normal brilliance.

Of course, no student should ever be allowed to be so excited, engaged, and challenged that they are allowed to run through a classroom. Imagine the chaos if we allowed that opportunity! We would be forever having conversations with parents about it. "I know that Kira can read novels on the 11th grade level, but she is going alarmingly fast. She is going to miss out on some excellent comprehension activities in the classroom. And what if there are no books available in the library at her reading level? We don't have the budget to buy more books. Why don't we bring her back down to earth, huh? Maybe a few picture books would be better—books with fewer words and fuzzy animals with big eyes. Let's let her catch her breath and calm down. What's the hurry, anyway?"

Gifted children, like all children, need to grow intellectually to thrive both academically and social-emotionally. "When a brain is engaged with meaningful material, motivation increases because the reward system is activated creating a surge of positive neurochemicals like dopamine and produces a cycle of reward and motivation" (Tetrault, p. 47). When gifted kids are running—both literally and figuratively—it's healthy. We need to stop asking "What's the hurry?" and start asking, "How can I help you hurry?"

Hit the Ground Running

The phrase, "hit the ground running" seems apt for gifted kids who often reach developmental milestones like crawling and walking earlier than other children. I see a stroller tipping forward and a gifted kid spilling out with feet already spinning in the air—gaining traction and sprinting away when their shoes touch the playground.

"Did you teach her that?"

"I didn't teach her that."

"How on earth did she know?"

"I don't have any idea. She just…knows…stuff. Happens all the time!"

Your gifted kid, driven by her physical intensities, bounces on couch cushions, tosses them to the floor so she can bound from one to the next.

"Can't touch the lava!" She leaps from one chair to the next. You hear a cracking noise coming from the arm of that expensive chair. "I crossed the chasm!"

"Where did she learn that word—*chasm*?"

"No idea. Yesterday, she told me that the scrape on her knee was *significant* but that she was willing to *endure it like a true warrior*."

She sprawls over edge of the recliner; apparently, it doesn't recline enough for her. You catch her squishing the backs of cushions as she lays across the top of the sofa in exactly the way you've asked her not to. It seems like you spend your life ready to dive with arms outstretched and catch her from a fall. It's exhausting…and all this while she is just watching a cartoon on television. Does she ever stop moving? Yes, while asleep, but your kid sleeps fewer hours than others, too.

What's the Hurry?

Working on individually-paced projects in my classroom, I rarely had to badger students to get to work; but sometimes I had to hold them back from getting started. Sometimes we needed to have a group meeting for important instructions or for discussing a social-emotional issue that had been boiling to the top. That's why I started hanging a yellow flag on days I needed the kids to hit the pause button at the beginning of class.

This yellow flag isn't actually a flag. It is a big sheet of construction paper that hangs down almost to eye level from the top of my doorway. Caution—yellow. Slow down. Wait. The kids know what it means, though it rarely actually stops the first kid entering the room. They seem to think that if they ignore it—it nearly hits them on the forehead as they walk through the door—that it may just go away. Who knows? Maybe Mr. Hess has mistakenly taped that big sheet of yellow construction paper into the middle of the doorway. Maybe he has really meant it for the last group. Surely, it's not meant for us!

"Yellow flag," I'd say, as the first few students walk through the door. I imagine I may even have spoken these words while standing a few feet inside the classroom with my arms folded.

"Really?"

"Yes."

"Aw…"

You'd think I'd punched a hole in their birthday balloon. The only consolation was "if I have to do it, at least everybody has to do it." The first few students would mirror my stance, announcing "yellow flag" in a stern voice to their classmates, who react in similar fashion to the disappointing delay of their dopamine hit. They slink over to the desks, some of them even actually sitting in a chair rather than on top of the desk, on the floor, or on a table.

Eyes downcast, an impatient tilt of the jaw, they seem to be saying, "So what's so important you have to interrupt me from the creation of the most amazing project in the entire history of the world and galaxy? Are you trying to ruin my life?"

Right Feet. Wrong Shoes.

One of the most poignant interactions I've had with a gifted child was the day a 4th grade girl was asked to switch her shoes onto the wrong feet in a classroom simulation about discrimination. The intentions were good on her teacher's part, but the result for this gifted girl—fully equipped with emotional sensitivities, her non-retractable cheetah's claws—bordered on traumatic.

I had come to the classroom to help with the simulation, and I arrived amidst a loud, chaotic, and confused disarray as children scrambled to switch their shoes. Kids were tumbling over one another in a small area of the classroom entryway—desks jammed into a line keeping students from entering the larger space of the classroom. Their teacher, normally quite calm and pleasant, was conducting the simulation in a loud and firm voice. Most of the children grinned and chattered excitedly. They knew something was up, and they were having fun with it. This was some excitement! What would happen next? Most kids reacted this way… but not Annie.

Once while I was leading a first grade reading group, I had allowed the rest of the class get a bit noisy (most likely a generous understatement). As someone at home with upper elementary, middle school, and high school, I don't have the well-developed ability to somehow keep five groups on task simultaneously. My colleagues who teach primary have figured this out, though, and I will forever stand in awe. I had asked a question to the small group of students sitting at the breakout table with me, and instead of hearing a response to my question from one particular gifted girl, she looked out at her energetic classmates, sunk into a sort of protective posture in which she covered her ears, closed her eyes tightly, and shook her head. "It's too much," she told me. In that moment, aside from feeling guilty that I hadn't managed the class very well, I saw the girl's gifted intensities physicalized. For gifted kids who feel the world so intensely, a noisy room can be too much. For Annie that day in her classroom, the noise, the chaos, her emotional sensitivity—a place that typically felt safe to her—and the physical intensity of shoes literally on the wrong feet, was too much to bear.

Annie wobbled into a standing position, shoes on the wrong feet, her face turning red, and then she froze in place, lifted her hands to hide her face, and began to cry. As her classmates playfully squabbled and laughed expectantly, Annie began sobbing uncontrollably. There was no solace or apology or quiet assurance from her teacher that it was OK, that she was just putting on a show for the simulation, that she never imagined it would so upset Annie. The intensities in the simulation were simply too much. Annie's wide-open sensitivities were simply too vulnerable. She felt the distress of others as well as her own, and the classroom chaos turned her upside down. My words, similar to the teacher's, offered no respite either. A hand gently on her shoulder, I offered to take Annie to my classroom as the rest of the class continued the simulation.

In the hallway, we stopped so that Annie could put her shoes back on the right feet. By the time we made it down the stairs to my room, her tears were mostly gone, and we could talk about what had happened.

"I came today just thinking it would be a normal day at school, a fun day, and then it all just fell apart. Why did this have to happen?"

I think of that day as emblematic for the life of gifted kids in school—how life in the classroom can sometimes seem like wearing shoes on the wrong feet, how some children accept this and enjoy it expectantly, how others become disoriented or even heartbroken. I think about how grateful I am that Annie had a safe space to come to, just down the stairs in my classroom. I think about the beauty of her emotional intensities and her inability to do anything but be herself—to feel all of it even if it was distressing. I hope she can always sprint through this world with the wind at her back.

As we grow older, however, we understand that the wind will not always be at our backs. We start to insulate ourselves against traumas both great and small. We've learned not to run the risk of *feeling it all.* We become weary fighting our way through headwinds. Gifted children, with their receptivity open wide, bared sensitivities, and enhanced emotional depth, have not learned to wrap themselves in layers. Cheetahs have to run. Gifted kids have to run. They are who they are, even when they are forced to wear their shoes on the wrong feet.

◇◇◇

One of my twice exceptional students, Easton, often wore his shoes on the wrong feet. It didn't seem to bother him. In our 2nd grade gifted and talented group, we were creating physical metaphors to illustrate different feelings one day. He sat silently and expressionless long after other kids had raced ahead with drawings showing the metaphors they would later build from craft items. I wondered if this metaphor project might be asking too much for this boy who is very literal in the way he views things, so I checked in on him a couple times, encouraging him. The rest of the class raced ahead. Still no movement from Easton. Finally, as I was on my way to his desk to help brainstorm an alternative way of expressing his understanding, he began drawing the flag of the United Nations. This flag would be his metaphor for "acceptance." His drawing was intricate and detailed, and I was impressed with how accurately a 2nd grader had drawn this complicated flag from memory.

"Wow! You were really thinking hard about that, weren't you?" I asked him.

"I was thinking long, but I wasn't thinking hard," he tells me, carefully choosing his words, "because first I had to remember everything about how it looks before I could draw it."

Sitting so very still, he had been running all along.

◇◇◇

Another 2nd grade boy, another twice exceptional student, another day, and we are creating stories. Our task is to draw a story board to plan our story. Eric has drawn one single picture in the first panel of his story board in the space of 40 minutes.

His classroom teacher sees flashes of brilliance from him, but she is also frustrated, working in a room of 25 students. "Many days, he is doing nothing. Nothing!"

As the group is leaving, I ask Eric if I can help him think of ideas for his story so he can work on it next time. Instead, Eric starts telling me the story that is inside his head—smiling at first and then laughing at the humorous situations his character will encounter. Well after his classmates have left my room, his story continues…and his laughter gains momentum and keeps running and running and running.

It is unclear why some gifted learners are diagnosed with slow processing speed. In Eric's case, I believe he becomes stuck on thoughts and ideas and wonderings. The class has moved on to the next several activities, but he is still wondering how a barometer works from the lesson about weather an hour before. "Perhaps," Duncan, Goodwin, Haas, and Wilson state, "because children's brains are works-in-progress, information pathways may be developing asychronously which may, at times, leave gifted individuals struggling to coordinate and communicate, as they trip over their own thoughts" (p. 2 in Greater Connectivity Across Brain Regions). It can be hard to choose where to run, after all, when you are invited to race in so many different directions.

◇◇◇

Another day and still more shoes and more asynchronicity. A first-grade boy—intensely brilliant—has licked the bottom of his shoe. I am happy to see that by the expression on his face that he will not do this again. Oh, well. Some kids just have to experience things before they learn them.

His brain works like a twelve-year-old's brain, but he is the size of a preschooler with similar social skills. His teacher tells me that he has at least one meltdown a day where he collapses on the floor in simulated agony—often over a minor mistake he has made on an assignment or in a refusal to transition from one activity to another. He spends most of his time smiling and laughing, though, and it's impossible not to like him for it.

While the class sits at their spots on the rug to listen to a story, he learns best while moving around and doing other stuff. He is listening even though he doesn't look like it, and the other kids seem to understand this and accept it, too. In my teacher's chair at the front of the group on the rug, I am reading a Junior Great Books story about a large and horrible snake, and when I get to the exciting part near the climax, he comes to stand directly in front of me, breathing in and out in visible expectation, and then laughs and falls to the floor when the story's humor hits him.

A week later, I run into him in the hallway (a common phenomenon, by the way; some of the most brilliant, gifted boys always seem to be out in the hallway every chance they get.) He smiles his enormous wide-open smile and waves at me. He has run all the way down to the end of the hallway when I see him spin around and run back toward me.

He stops and catches his breath, holds up a finger to make a point. "That was a really good story!" he is compelled to tell me.

But what about those kids who are running but not smiling, I wonder.

Running and Running and Running

"Oh, Terrance is bright for sure. I'm not sure he is gifted, though," his teacher says. And then she adds, "And he has anger issues."

"Oh?"

Terrance, a 7-year-old boy, has laser beam focus. He insists on explaining how he has arrived at each answer in the nonverbal ability test I am administering to him. I try to tell him that he doesn't have to explain; he just has to choose an answer, but he keeps explaining. I decide to let him go.

Leaning forward intently, he points to and explains every answer correctly and logically until he gets to the very last question. It's incredible. He has not guessed at one single answer. For the last question, he still does not guess. Instead, he sits back, resigned, and tells me, "I don't know this one." He has scored in the 99.9^{th} percentile.

"Anger issues?" I ask for further information from his teacher.

"Yes, I notice it when I don't call on him. He wants to shout out, but I don't let him. He is impatient waiting for others. He gets upset when other kids don't see things his way."

This, too, is how asynchronicity runs. Terrance's brain makes connections only 0.1% of the population can make. Full of intensities, he might seem angry at times. You can feel it. It can become a bit alarming—these waves of energy barely held inside this boy. His brain sprints at record speed—jumps synapses like an Olympic hurdler. His emotional control, though, is that of a typical 8-year-old boy.

◇◇◇

Ash, a first grader who understood negative numbers in kindergarten, is invited along with all the other first graders who finish math assignments early to write numbers on a large register tape roll. Their instructions are to keep writing numbers as high as they can go.

It's fun unrolling the tape and writing numbers. Ash's tape soon stretches across the classroom and then out the door and into the hallway. Though some of his numbers are written backwards, he still hasn't come to the end after weeks of finishing assignments early. The numbers just keep coming. At age six, he loves doing this. It has become an amusing contest with a couple other gifted students in his classroom to see how far he can stretch the tape. He wonders, could he make it to the moon? For now, he is delighted.

The novelty will wear off eventually. "Studies show that once a person masters a skill, brain activity decreases and is dulled each time the mastered skill is repeated" (Haeir, Richard J. et al, as cited by Tetrault, p. 47). If Ash isn't offered new challenges on a regular basis, he will stop running. If new challenges aren't offered, he will learn how to disengage to avoid boredom—will seek new places outside of school curriculum to engage his creativity. The neurology of growth and learning—neuroplasticity—requires appropriate challenge. "In study after study it has been found that new neural connections are not formed unless the material encountered is difficult enough to require some work and struggle" (Miller, p. 20-21).

◇◇◇

In 5th grade, Eli has constructed a car entirely of his own invention. It's made from craft sticks, dowels and wooden wheels from the classroom's craft bin. He has assembled a battery and small electric motor as an engine. Today, he is literally running with the challenge. He laughs and chases the car across the classroom to unclip the battery from the motor. "I need an ignition switch… or maybe a remote!" His mother cannot afford to supply him and his brother with such craft items. Eli will stop 'running' if no one can provide resources to continue to stretch his inventor's imagination and skills.

◇◇◇

Another girl and another car. Angel, a 2nd grader, carefully and quietly creates crafty, artistic designs for her *Hot Wheels* obstacle course in the GT group, where she stands out among 22 gifted seven- and eight-year-olds. Many days, she arrives late to school. She misses many days entirely, having told her teacher that her mom has been sick.

"Do we get to keep these cars?" she asks me quietly. "I would like to build more things at home, but I don't have a toy car."

"I haven't decided," I tell her. I had previously thought that I would use these little cars again and again for other projects, and with my limited budget, it probably wouldn't be prudent to keep replenishing my classroom supply.

At the end of the day when the other students are out the door, I call to her—*Hot Wheel* car held out in my hand. "Hey, don't forget to take your car home!" She smiles and slips it inside her backpack.

I wanted to make sure she can keep running.

◇◇◇

Rory has self-published a novel (with a little graphic design and editing help from her mother) of more than 200 pages, in the 4th grade. Her classmates purchase her novel online and leave 5-star reviews. She happily autographs copies. Her standardized testing numbers do not technically qualify her for the gifted and talented program in our school even though she is running far, far ahead of her classmates. If her school or district do not understand it is more important to serve gifted kids than to identify them, she too will be forced to do all of her 'running' outside of school.

◇◇◇

Robert, another 4th grader, has not completed his illustrated space-themed ABCs book assignment by the time it is due. He has only made it to letter D, actually. This book is not "A for Asteroid" and "B for Black Hole." His book is richly and colorfully illustrated and is full of amazing facts—detailed descriptions he is pulling from his own head. He is running deep, deep into the curriculum without ever finishing an assignment. His teacher understands this, is delighted and encouraging. If Robert can't run with his talents and passions—if he can't run deeper or wider or runs into teachers who don't understand his gifts—he may be officially judged an underachiever someday, instead of a 4th grader who didn't finish an ABC book (because he vastly exceeded the parameters of the assignment).

◇◇◇

Estefania, a 7th grader, is gifted both intellectually and as a cross-country runner. Her mother explains that her daughter sails through school but at home agonizes about mistakes and upcoming projects. She can't seem to live up to her own standards—thinks the world is watching her every move and expecting perfection. One of the "8 Great Gripes of GT Kids" shared by Galbraith (2013) is "Parents, teachers, and even our friends expect too much of us. We're supposed to get A's and do our best all the time" (p. 24). This gripe, however, seems to pale in comparison to the sometimes-impossible standards to which gifted learners hold themselves.

All season in cross-country, she has finished first every time. At the city cross-country championships, she is passed in the last 100 meters of the race. Instead of finishing second in a tough division of middle schoolers, she simply stops and collapses onto the grass, refusing to go on. If we cannot help Estefania learn to be forgiving to herself, if we cannot help her feel safe to be less than perfect and to understand that she is lovable and unique and wonderfully imperfect for who she is, then she will either stop running (literally and figuratively), or begin to run only in the middle of the pack where she can go unnoticed.

◇◇◇

Rae, an expressive girl who is a creative writer and delightfully funny in her off-the-cuff comments, must be convinced to join the speech team in 6th grade. By the summer of 7th grade, Rae has won the middle school national championship in dramatic interpretation of literature. Not finding a connection to coaches and classmates in high school, she has stopped competing by 10th grade. In 7th grade, she had found a key component to gifted identity: affiliation. "To affiliate, people need to be valued for who they are—for their uniqueness, talent, specialness" (Mahoney, p. 6). Her affiliation gone, we wonder if she is no longer running. Is she standing still, or has she found a new affiliation and developed a new affinity?

◇◇◇

Tabitha's transcript notes that in kindergarten she "has done a great job academically" but is still working on "independent skills and social interactions." As a 1st grader, the teacher notes, "She is a very social girl and enjoys interacting with her peers." In 2nd grade, though it is noted she is well-liked by her peers, sometimes she is "spacey" and needs to "make sure she is on task." Neuroscience research shows three brain networks actively connect during deep creative thought. One network, the default mode network, is activated during mind wandering and may explain "spacey" behaviors (Tetrault, p. 99). At third grade, our gifted girl "has a tendency to frequently observe the environment around her and therefore needs a little redirection." Her teacher expresses confidence that she will "adapt nicely to her new teachers and classmates."

At her new school, Tabitha is the quietest girl in the classroom. She has found one good friend, though—a girl on the autism spectrum who has trouble regulating her emotions. Tabi is a calm presence for her friend. She spends her time filling notebooks with cartoon drawings that are expressive and full of life, and this notebook is the reason her teacher refers Tabi for gifted testing. In an open-ended project, Tabi's three-dimensional constructions are full of life and creatively amusing. She smiles to herself while she is carefully crafting them. Before the school year ends, Tabitha moves away again, and though her teachers write enthusiastic narratives to accompany her identification paperwork in her cumulative file, they worry that this newly quiet girl will not "get found" in her new school.

Running on Water

For a very short time growing up a gifted kid, I didn't merely run. I actually ran on water. Messing around one day at the age of about 9, I discovered that my toy GI Joe rubber raft fit perfectly onto my foot. I had two of those rafts. I stepped both feet inside of them. It gave me an idea.

The next day at the swimming pool, I stepped my feet into the toy rubber rafts at the edge of the pool, wiggled around to make sure they fit snugly, and smiled with a secret knowledge. This was going to be amazing. I couldn't believe that no one had ever thought of this before. One toy raft on each foot. I was about to run across the surface of the swimming pool.

I looked around to see if anyone was watching. They didn't seem to be watching, but they soon would. "Whoa! Look! Do you see that?! Look at that kid running across the water! That's kid Jesus!"

I would wave to them casually as I strode across the pool—the bright orange GI Joe rafts barely churning up the water under my feet. "Hey, nice day, isn't it? Oh, don't mind me," I'd smile and wave modestly, "I'm just out for a stroll across the pool… walking on water, you know."

Poolside, I stepped into my raft shoes, splashing down through the water's surface to the first of the concrete stairs in the shallow end. In that moment I had learned a powerful lesson about the nature of buoyancy. I looked around to see if anyone was watching, and thankfully they were not. I tossed the toy rafts to the side with my towel, 30 cents rolled up securely inside so that I could buy a Three Musketeers candy bar later, and dived into the pool.

You might be thinking that somehow I had failed, but I had not. I had run on water, if only in my mind. Imagining about it all the evening before and in the morning until the pool opened, I had enjoyed running across the water—effortless running, a letting go of this world and a brief glimpse at the beauty of perfection.

Years later in another water scene, I would snap a photo of my daughter running away from the Atlantic surf crashing on the beach at Montauk behind her. A photo is a magical capturing of time. In this photo, midstride, my daughter's feet don't touch the ground. Her smile is pure joy. The part of the photo we do not see—the part that time does not capture—is the moment when the wave would catch up to her and roll her head-over-heels onto the sand. I am happy to say, however, that she had parents there who comforted her, who held her afterwards, and who made sure she felt safe. She had someone in her life who would encourage her to step back out into the surf again.

Please remember, though, the part of the scene where her feet did not touch the ground, the part where she was not just running but also flying, the part where even if it were in her imagination, she could have been walking on water. Please remember when the same thing has happened to you or your child.

Gifted kids not only run. Sometimes they fly.

References

Daniels, Susan, and Piechowski, Michael, Eds. 2009. *Living with Intensity*. Scottsdale, AZ: Great Potential Press.

Duncan, Sharon. Goodwin, Corin. Haase, Joanna. Wilson, Sarah. Accessed June 2021. Neuroscience of giftedness. *Gifted Research and Outreach*. www.gro-gifted.org/the-neuroscience-of-giftedness/

Gatto-Walden, Patricia. 2018. Colorado Association for Gifted and Talented state conference.

Galbraith, J. (2013). *The survival guide for gifted kids* (3rd ed.). Free Spirit.

Mahoney, Andrews S. Accessed June 2021. In search of gifted identity: from abstract concept to workable counseling constructs (a series of articles including Greater connectivity across brain regions) . *Counseling the Gifted*. www.counsellingthegifted.com

Miller, Erin M. Clinkenbeard, Pamela R. 2021. Find the signal and ignoring the noise. *Parenting for High Potential*. National Association for Gifted Children. Vol 10. Issue 2.

Tetrault, Nicole. 2020. *Insight into a bright mind*. Goshen, KY: Gifted Unlimited LLC.

Tolan, Stephanie. 1996. *Is it a cheetah?* http://www.stephanietolan.com/is_it_a_cheetah.htm

Chapter 3
Fully Oneself

Surfing a Wave of Wonderfulness first appeared in the
National Association of Gifted Children blog at NAGC.org

This is How Boys are Tough first appeared in the
Supporting the Emotional Needs of Gifted Library at Sengifted.org

What Gifts Do You Bring?

This fall, a colleague pointed to Joy Lawson Davis's *Bright, Black, and Talented* book on my desk. "I'm not sure I get it," she said. It was a sincere question—the sort of honest and vulnerable question Glenn Singleton encourages all of us to ask in his book, *Courageous Conversations About Race.* I stumbled through a rambling answer that might have hit home a few times, missed the mark widely by other estimations, but kept me thinking throughout the day. Though my response was heartfelt, I wish I could have articulated my thoughts more clearly—that I could have said something more poignant and true or at least have been able to articulate the questions in my own mind.

When a child sits down to take a standardized test based on national norms, not only are they sitting down with their unique neurological markers, but they also carry with them a lifetime of experiences. What gifts do they bring to the chair in which they sit, and what gifts will the test—the educational system—not allow them to show?

Do the people around them engage in conversations about relationships, justices and injustices alike? When they pass a historical marker, does a parent read the inscription aloud? Do they pull a stepladder up to the open hood of a car and watch their uncle change a carburetor? Do they spend weekends visiting museums? Are they valued for their verve and storytelling abilities, or are they valued for their obedience? Does an adult expect them to remain silent? Which of these skills does a standardized test measure?

Is their house filled with books, or are they the surrogate parent for younger siblings from the end of the school day until six p.m.? Do they know the legends of those who've come before them? How do we measure the response one feels in one's heart when such a connection is made to a past generation? Are they praised for competitive zeal and individual accomplishments, or for their collaboration and teamwork? Do they see their parents pull together resources to make it to the end of a month? Are they taught to stand out, or are they encouraged to honor traditions? How much laughter is in their lives? How many words of anger have been seeded in their hearts? Whose culture gets to assign value?

Do they wear an apartment key around their neck? Have they ever helped deliver a baby calf, felt the heat of a mid-day sun on their shoulders next to a corn field? Do they feel unconditional love? Are they sitting down to take that test with a full stomach, or was their last meal served the day before in the school cafeteria? Will they return home to their own space in their own temperature-controlled room, or do they wonder where home will be that night? Have they ever travelled abroad? Do they know the power of a thunderbird flapping its wings? Have they ever stood outside at night and seen the stars?

Whose "data midpoint" are we measuring? Our best achievement tests are limited by what we value inside a school and a school system, inside a society, inside a mainstream culture. We face a challenge to identify equitably our underserved populations. As Dr. Gilman Whiting referred to it in his keynote address at the 2020 NAGC National Conference, "compounding adversities—Black, ELL, living in a major city, poverty—make this process of identification even more difficult." We, as educators, he goes on to say, are the gatekeepers, and "our compassion is an absolute imperative." An 85th percentile means different things to different people in different neighborhoods and in different schools. In gifted education, we are charged to understand and serve the children whose abilities stretch the system—no matter if that system is in Garfield Park or Morrill, Nebraska; in Cherry Hills, Colorado or on the Wind River Reservation in Wyoming. We can't ever assume an 85 is just a number in a database. That 85 is a whole child, and as teachers, we strive to see that whole child. We will do everything we can to help the whole child succeed—academically and social-emotionally. That's what we do. That's who we are. That's the best answer I could have given to my colleague's question.

So We Are Wondering if Our Gifted Child has ADHD…

That's exactly what the parents leaned forward and whispered about their daughter Lilly as they sat down for parent-teacher conferences. Lilly had already dashed off into the fun parts of my classroom in search of the puzzle cabinet while her kindergarten sister sat down quietly to listen to our conversation. "She doesn't seem to focus sometimes. You start talking to her, and before you know it, she is wondering about and asking about twelve other things including strawberry shortcake."

Mom and Dad are smiling at their own comments, playing verbal ping pong and bouncing stories back and forth. Their eyes are lit. They love their quirky kid. "For example, I will be reading aloud to her at home," Dad says, "and the next thing I know she is up and wandering around, fiddling with things on the bookshelf. I'll stop and tell her that if she really doesn't want me to read to her that I can stop. But, no, that's not it. She knows everything I've been saying, and can recite back every detail from the story."

Lilly is in all of my gifted groups for her grade level—having scored 99+ on the verbal portion of the Kaufman Brief Intelligence Test (KBIT), as well as 99+ on the Test of Mathematical Abilities for Gifted Students (TOMAGS). Her first-grade classroom was next door the previous year, and even though my school doesn't typically identify gifted first graders, her teacher had often sent her to my room for extra challenges. This year, as a part of the gifted literacy group, Lilly often has a project in full swing on her desktop (or hidden away inside her desk) while the rest of the class discusses stories in the group. I don't know how many times I've witnessed a gifted kid secretly reading under their desktop or drawing or building something when they are supposed to be doing something else. Lilly's desk is filled with construction paper and markers and craft items that have accumulated throughout the semester. She doesn't seem to be the least bit worried that I will think she is not listening, because she knows I know she is! In a system in which gifted kids spend up to one-fourth or one-half of their time waiting for others to catch up, even my gifted class is too slow for her. Lilly starts creative assignments before I've finished introducing them. Her products tumble off her desk and onto the floor where she has extra space. Neat card-stock patterns I've provided as an aid for little second-grader hands get ignored for her own patterns and creations which are much more detailed and exhibit much more flair than the ones I've provided.

Talking with Lily's parents, all eyes around the table are huge, intent, and focused as we discuss misdiagnosis and intensities of the gifted. Dad's and Little Sister's eyes are quietly expectant. Mom's eyes are huge, too, and full of energy. She is nodding and laughing and finishing others' sentences for them, and when I suggest that if she reads *Living with Intensities*—she smiles and finishes my thought for me—"I might even learn something about myself when I read it."

"The gifted child's characteristics of intensity, sensitivity, impatience, and high motor activity can easily be mistaken for ADHD (J. Webb, Amend, N. Webb, Goerss, Beljan, and Olenchak, 2011). As Dr. Ed Amend points out in his chapter on misdiagnosis of the gifted, in *Living with Intensity*, behaviors of psychomotor overexcitability—an excess of energy, rapid speaking, and restlessness—are also behaviors descriptive of ADHD.

It should be be clear, however, that some gifted children are twice-exceptional, i.e., gifted as well as challenged with an attentional disorder. How do we tell the difference? One key area of clarity is the situation in which such behaviors are present. Attentional disorders are persistent and widespread across life situations, but gifted overexcitabilities tend to be situational. Lilly's 99+ percentiles on KBIT and TOMAGS were not mirrored by her Cognitive Abilities Test (CogAT) scores, where she scored as low as the 73rd percentile on the verbal battery. Having known Lilly for a year before she took the CogAT, I knew that 73% could not possibly be accurate. Her test scores indicated a wide confidence band. In other words, Lilly had answered several questions incorrectly that a student in the 73rd percentile would typically have answered correctly. Conversely, she had also answered several questions correctly that a student scoring in the 73rd percentile would be expected to answer incorrectly. In short, her response patterns pointed to possible inaccuracies. How could this happen? I had a pretty good idea. As the school district's universal screener, our teachers proctor the 2nd grade CogAT to rooms full of 20 to 30 students. In this format, a class is moved through the test at the same pace—that is, at the pace of the slowest responder. Because Lilly answers questions at lightning speed, she had most likely lost patience with the process. Sure enough, her 99+ scores emerged on tests in which she worked at her own pace. In fact, she had finished the TOMAGS so quickly that I thought she hadn't even tried.

Misdiagnosis can change the course of an education. An education can change the course of a life. Professionals with little experience in giftedness, despite all their best intentions, may help orchestrate a path that is counterproductive to growth, and at its worst, damaging for years to come. "An inaccurate diagnosis may lead to a view of the behaviors as something to eliminate rather than something to embrace and help grow" (Amend, p. 87). Through the lens of a classroom teacher, Lilly's mess around and inside her desk is a problem. Through the lens of giftedness, Lilly's mess of a school desk and the floor around it are beautiful because they are signs of a complex inchoate intelligence seeking the tools of focused expression. The problem is that the classroom teacher defaults to the idea that it is a problem.

The next time we find ourselves thinking that our gifted children are going too far, over-reacting, or pouring on emotions just a little too much, perhaps we should remember that in squelching the overexcitabilities we may be missing out on a unique child's world seeking self-expression and growth. Gifted kids need to be allowed to be "too much." It's who they are.

For More Information and Support

NAGC Supporting Twice Exceptional Students: http://nagc.org/supporting-twice-exceptional-students

NAGC's White Paper on Twice Exceptionality: http://www.nagc.org/sites/default/files/Position%20Statement/twice%20exceptional.pdf

Parenting for High Potential, "Twice Exceptional Focus Issue," Vol 8, Number 4, December 2019.

SENG Misdiagnosis Initiative: http://www.sengifted.or/misdiagnosis-intiative

References

Amend, Edward R. *Living with Intensity*. Daniels, Susan, and Piechowski, Michael, Eds. Scottsdale, AZ: Great Potential Press. 2009.

Webb, James T., Amend, Edward R., Webb, Nadia E., Goerss, Jean, Beljan, Paul, and Olenchak. *Misdiagnosis and Dual Diagnosis of Gifted Children*. SENGifted.org, September 13, 2011.

A Virtuoso

I will forever remember her as The Caped Savannah. According to her second-grade teacher, she swept into her classroom one spring day with a wool blanket draped around her shoulders like a cape. Raising the cape in front of her eyes, she silently peered from behind it—her bright eyes shining—and darted from doorway to closet door. She emerged from under a desktop and crept from the group table to the computers. On that day, The Caped Savannah was truly thriving—virtuosity was unabashedly on display for an imaginary audience. She wasn't fretting about finding anyone's approval or meeting anyone's expectations. No thoughts of whether she would be judged, assessed, encouraged, or discouraged crossed her mind.

She was simply and authentically her true and wonderful self. That spring day our Caped Savannah was thriving.

Instead of choosing a cape, many of our gifted kids choose a cloak. Just peeking out, just letting in enough light to safely navigate the world, wrapping themselves up to protect themselves from failures, disappointments, or unmet and impossible expectations—typically their own. That's where many of our gifted kids are hiding. Most of the gifted students I've worked with over the past 35 years are high achievers. Most seem to be getting along quite well socially. Most go from assignment to assignment, class to class, with barely a ripple of disturbance on the surface. They've carefully crafted their path in that way. I'm not so sure, however, that they are truly thriving.

I encountered an intriguing definition of what it means to thrive at a leadership training: thriving involves "an exchange of virtuosities and vulnerabilities that allows people to do their best work." *Virtuosity* is defined as one's true and transparent talents—talents so ingrained and so unplanned that we know of our virtuosity only through evidence we get from others who know us well. *Vulnerability* is defined as being susceptible and assailable—an atmosphere of challenge where one finds opportunity to contribute one's virtuosity. If this defines thriving, then our cloaked perfectionist gifted learners rarely thrive.

Sure, a perfectionist may do very well very often, may in fact accomplish long lists of wonderful things, may *wow* the world, delight their loved ones, may cause us to stand back with pleasure and thank the universe for their presence. They are a virtuoso to everyone except their own self. A perfectionist rarely believes in his or her own virtuosity. A perfectionist is always doubting their own virtuosity, worrying that they will lose it, or that they never had it in the first place. Because of this doubt it is no wonder that a perfectionist is never truly vulnerable—is always a bit on guard—and thus never truly thrives. Here is a simple test to discover if you or a loved one is a perfectionist. Just express their virtuosity to them honestly and sincerely, and listen for them to qualify it, deny it, or fail to comment at all. "You are so sincere in everything you do," you might say.

An immediate response, barely hesitating. "Well…not always. I'm not so sure that's true," comes their reply.

One of my gifted 5th grade students never handed in assignments; instead, she handed in apologies. She was sure I that would be disappointed, but I was usually very impressed. Seven years later as a senior in high school, she would be recognized as one of our community's best and brightest teenagers. I hope she took pride in the award—not secretly or ashamedly, but joyously and obviously. I hope she didn't apologize for it.

In Reducing Levels of Perfectionism in Gifted and Talented Youth, the authors cite mindfulness practices as having positive effects on improved attentional control and self-awareness, increased academic performance, increased emotional regulation, increased metacognitive awareness, and increased awareness of feelings and reactions to current situations. More specifically, their program, in which middle school gifted students were taught mindful responses to perfectionist tendencies, "reported significantly lower levels of self-prescribed perfectionism" (p. 325). Humans hold powerful reactions to language, most strongly, perhaps, to the language inside our own minds. Mindfulness helps provide us with awareness to intercept negative self-talk, to slow down our thinking and examine the words we speak to ourselves, to stop listening to the apologies we are already creating for our efforts before anyone else has even seen it. Mindful practices help our gifted perfectionists breathe and accept truths about their virtuosities. This confidence may lead to the opportunity afforded by vulnerabilities to open the world to their potential.

As teachers and friends and parents, let's remember that behind the cloak of a gifted learner shines a bright and beautiful mind—often unsure of itself, often hesitant to take the risk lest the shadows of failure descend. Most simply, as mentors and loved ones, as teachers and counsellors, we can help students thrive, not through a grand and planned re-programming, but through honest compassion, and by practicing honest acceptance which allows a safety zone for susceptible and assailable vulnerability. Let's help build healthy intrapersonal as well as interpersonal relationships. Let's help build healthy futures by building a vast storehouse of acceptance. Let's help fill classrooms and households alike with Caped Savannahs.

References

Olton-Weber, Sophia. Hess, Robyn and Ritchotte, Jennifer A. 2020. *Gifted Child Quarterly*. Vol 64(4) p. 310-330.

Surfing a Wave of Wonderfulness

Assuredly this conference with Maddie's parents will be quick and pleasant. Maddie is a wonderful kid—pleasant, creative and artistic, mature, and driven toward success.

We check the boxes on our way down the parent-teacher conference list, exchange pleasantries and accolades about Madeline, and as I had predicted, her parents will be quickly on their way.

"What a wonderful young lady!" Check.

"Your daughter is so very mature!" Check.

"A leader!" Check.

"I love your daughter! I wish I had a full classroom of your daughters!" Check.

"We think we may keep her!" they smile. Check.

"OK, then…" I smile. Check.

"So, we guess we'll be going then…" Check.

"But…just one more thing." Madeline's parents are getting up from their chairs to leave and then sit back down.

"Yes?"

There are some things I hope you will help me keep an eye on.

"Oh?"

◇◇◇

Everything seems to come so very easily and quickly to the Madelines in our classrooms. Most likely, school is a breeze—a place for the Maddies to shine brilliantly every day. They've grown accustomed not to just success, but to a very quick brand of academic success. To these students, this ready-made academic level of accomplishment is a deep and true part of their *normal*. They've never known any other way.

But I'm worried that Maddie and students like her will believe this *normal* is what learning is all about, that learning means everything comes easily almost all of the time. Part of my job as a gifted resource teacher is to ensure Maddie and other gifted learners are challenged; but many gifted specialists maintain the gifted *normal* without providing challenge for growth. In an educational system which often places giftedness at the end of a long list of needs, I'm worried that students like Maddie will be very hard on themselves when healthy challenges prevent them finding immediate success.

We reassure students like Maddie how wonderful they are on a daily basis. Of course we do! We all are guilty of the praise—even those of us who know better. Despite the best advice from researchers like Carol Dweck who urge us to be specific in our comments, to focus on behaviors and not outcomes, and to praise effort over results, it's still so easy to find oneself lavishing praise on the Maddies of the school precisely because they are wonderful in so many ways. You know you shouldn't have that wedge of cheesecake. But there it is…right in front of you and looking so very wonderful!

Ease of achievement and success and praise become an addictive combination. Why wouldn't they? Who wouldn't want to feel that way all of the time?

In this way, some gifted kids surf atop a wave of wonderfulness.

Atop that wave, we forget what it feels like to have that little icky feeling in our stomachs we feel when a challenge presents itself. That icky feeling can easily be confused with a feeling of failure. A student like Madeline might think that if she doesn't *get it* not only quickly but also easily, then she has failed. Yuck. That icky feeling needs to go away, and the easiest way to make it go away is to avoid it.

Our Madelines start to think they are only valuable—literally, only loveable—when life is flowing easily and they are riding high atop that wave. This isn't to say these students will not accept challenge. They will! But the challenges they choose tend to be safe challenges…challenges which are practically certain to be met with a little hard work and dedication applied to them. Or the challenges might be challenges completed away from the eyes of others, on the student's own terms, at their own pace, and without risk of judgement. Challenge met, and no one was there to see me fail. In the end, the teacher will still put the "A" in the gradebook. (An "A minus" may actually be seen as a failure.) Perhaps these challenges shouldn't be regarded as challenges at all.

◇◇◇

Maddie's parents and I discuss *the wave of wonderfulness*. We listen to one another, express our concerns, and then a brief silence follows.

Maddie's mother says finally, "That's me."

"What do you mean?'

"I have never wanted to let anybody down either. And that's our daughter, too. The other night, Maddie lied to me about brushing her teeth. I'm thinking, 'seriously? You're going to lie about brushing your teeth?' But it was a failure to her, and she didn't want to admit it."

This exchange and reaction are very real to me. I've been in that perfectionist bubble many times myself. I still find myself defaulting to perfectionist feelings even though I understand where they come from, and even though I have been teaching social-emotional lessons about perfectionism for more than a decade. I still find myself worrying about the most ridiculous things—like somehow my wife won't love me if I don't do precisely the most wonderful thing, or if she disagrees with me about something. It's laughable on the outside, and I manage to laugh the thoughts away most of the time, but deep down inside these feelings are very real. No matter how much I understand my own perfectionism, it's difficult to let it go. I am like many of the kids I teach: perfectionism is our *factory pre-set*.

A perfectionist is ruled by an invisible and imaginary panel of judges. These judges are very stern. They are very exacting. They never *ever* miss a thing. They are unforgiving. The worst of it, though, is that these judges express the same warning over and over, "How could anyone love you if you let them down?" And the worst thing is we believe them. This is how a perfectionist falls off the wave.

The popular notion is to think of perfectionism as a Type A personality—uncompromising and exacting, holding others to an impossible standard, but perfectionism is not about that at all. Perfectionism is all about holding ONESELF to impossible standards, not about holding others to those standards. Perfectionism can be pervasive, and in the end it's much less about *doing* well than it is about *feeling* well. Even with forgetting to brush our teeth or not doing the exact, precise most wonderful thing, somewhere deep inside there is a fear that we won't be loveable anymore.

I have a vivid memory from kindergarten. It was some time in the spring of the school year. I had held it together all afternoon at school and all the way home on the bus, but in the safety of my own home and in the presence of my mother, the wave broke, and I came crashing down—sprawled out on the kitchen linoleum and crying uncontrollably. Why? That day I had failed to get a "star" on my paper. I was incorrect on two questions. Yes, seriously…I had been surfing the wave of wonderfulness, a star atop every paper, since August! In retrospect, this not only says a lot about perfectionism and gifted kids but also a lot about boys and moms.

Maddie's parents and I are winding down our discussion now. It really is time to end the conference. We have reached a consensus—a very important consensus we will take with us.

- ❍ Gifted kids are a joy. Check.
- ❍ Gifted kids need to be challenged. Check.
- ❍ Gifted kids need to feel—not failure exactly—but the challenge of trying, failing, re-grouping, and trying again. Check.
- ❍ Gifted kids need to understand that failure is natural and inevitable and that they are loveable even when they feel they have failed. Check.
- ❍ I've taught more than a hundred Maddies over a long career now—a long list of wonderful, gifted girls and boys. Classrooms full of them are a true privilege, but gifted kids need support like all kids need support. They don't simply "do OK if we just leave them alone." Check.
- ❍ Gifted kids are, after all, just kids too. Check.

We have to realize that even when we are surfing a wave of wonderfulness, we are still riding on top of an ocean. It is an ocean that is at once deep and perilous and sometimes murky with the unknown. But it is also beautiful and powerful and deeply, deeply authentic.

Check.

This is How Boys are Tough

Lucas, a 3rd grade student, has missed a day of school because of a stomachache. He returns on Thursday and Friday but manages to stay inside for recess. His stomach hurts all weekend, and he doesn't want to go back to school on Monday. On Monday morning, his mom discovers the cause of the stomachache. Another boy in his grade has been taunting Lucas at recess, and he does not want to go back to school *ever again*. "I don't understand why someone would treat someone else like that," he tells his mother.

◇◇◇

Third grader Nolan runs the last few strides into the classroom. He perches atop a desk, impatient for instructions and eager to get started on a project. "What are we going to do today?" He interrupts. He hushes his classmates with that loud *boy* voice my teaching colleagues know all too well at this age. "Come on, guys! Listen up! Listen up so we can get started! It's not fair that the other class has gotten to start on their projects already!"

◇◇◇

Jamison competes in gymnastics. He has been repeatedly warned not to perform a flip from atop the bench on the playground, yet he can't seem to resist. This parkour move from the bench is not a good model for other 4th graders who do not share Jamison's strength or training. Later at recess, rough play on everyone's part has led to a stern lecture before the line of students is allowed to return to class. A half hour later, Jamison has asked permission to leave his classroom so he can speak to the playground monitor. He wants the opportunity to apologize for his and the entire 4th grade's behavior.

◇◇◇

Though these three boys are navigating life quite differently in some ways, they share two strong characteristics: they are gifted learners, and they have tremendous leadership potential. Gifted boys have the intellectual capacity to understand that one way of being tough might be to show empathy. They often carry the emotional intensity to feel empathy beyond other boys, and if they are not afraid to experience these feelings, then such gifted boys possess a tremendous potential to make a positive impact as leaders. No, they won't explain to other 9- and 10-year-old boys about empathy. They won't pull a peer aside and have a heart-to-heart chat. Boy leadership is much simpler than that. It's as simple as being tough enough to be kind and inclusive and accepting of others. It's as simple as being tough enough to let generosity show. It's as simple as letting others be witness to your positive behavior on the playground, at lunch time, and inside the classroom. We need only a few boys with *high boy status* to start that trend—maybe an older boy, a boy who is already a leader through athletic talent, a boy who knows how to make others laugh, or maybe a male teacher.

We all know the gifted boy who is overflowing with vocabulary and verbal details about any number of topics—depending on what show he has recently seen on The Discovery Channel or what video he watched on YouTube. I am willing to bet, however, that the overflowing vocabulary and piles of details don't have much to do with feelings and emotions. Gifted boys—like all boys—may struggle with the expression of empathy and the words to express feelings. Those tendencies don't mean a gifted boy's capacity to feel empathy is diminished: muted, perhaps, but still ever-present. In a society which chooses to define male toughness through acts of strength and bravery and bravado, gifted boys—especially sensitive to the world around them—must be given permission for a full range of feelings. They must be shown there are a variety of ways to be tough, and that emotional strength is a valid form of courage.

Gifted boys must understand that the sensitivity and intensity through which they experience life is shared by other boys like them. *Yes, you belong. Yes, others are like you.* When these understandings are in place, even our 8–12-year-old gifted boys can develop strong leadership skills—if not by overt expressions of leadership, then by becoming positive role models for their friends, in their classrooms, and as a part of their school communities. When we read Kindlon and Thompson's *Raising Cain: Protecting the Social-Emotional Lives of Boys* through the lens of gifted education, we come away with even more poignant insights. When gifted boys understand that "courage and empathy are the sources of real strength in life" (p. 249), then they will possess the tremendous potential to make a positive impact.

Boy Talk

For some reason, the kitchen frequently became our meeting place after ball games and sports practices. The best conversations I had with my gifted son were standing side by side in the kitchen, both of us leaning against the counter and gazing ahead at—well—nothing, really. We talked about teammates and games and coaches—what we liked and didn't like, what looked like success and what looked like disappointment. There were often emotions expressed in those conversations, and many of the conversations went well beyond sports…but it was a rare instance when we talked directly about feelings. Feelings were understood, implied, inferred—not directly addressed. My son trusted me, and we both understood the *boy language* would take care of itself. I did not orchestrate these conversations as a teacher or as a dad and mentor. Somehow, they just felt right for both of us.

As teachers and parents, we must remember that we can't easily talk directly to boys about emotions and feelings. We must remember that unless we can frame social-emotional lessons in a manner in which boys will be open and responsive, we will not reach a receptive audience. I teach 30 elementary school boys in my gifted program each week. At ages 8-12, puberty and *the culture of cruelty* for these boys are just around the corner, and the stakes are about to be raised. The culture of cruelty all boys endure will be a time when being different from other boys in words or actions is treading a perilous ledge. This is particularly perilous for gifted boys who may already feel like something must be wrong with them. As Thompson and Barker state in *It's a Boy*, "A boy's ability to survive the culture of cruelty has everything to do with his emotional resources" (p. 89).

As the adults who love and nurture gifted boys, what do we do? We do not need to stand aside and accept any version of a cruel world. In the last year I taught students on a daily basis, at least 12 of 30 of my elementary-aged gifted boys possessed both the qualities and status to be leaders in their classrooms and beyond, and all 30 of them expressed the sensitivity to be aware of the culture around them. With this awareness, these boys and *all* boys, need to know quite clearly: *You are OK. You will be safe being exactly who you are.*

Through social-emotional instruction in gifted groups, we want boys to understand that their feelings of empathy are shared by other boys. Here again, we have Thompson and Barker stating their findings so eloquently: "The greatest gift to a boy's identity is a boy like himself, who confirms that he is all right" (p. 204). Let's take advantage of the intense loyalty boys at this age feel for one another and let this synergy carry boys forward outside of the gifted groups. Armed with understanding and bolstered by acceptance of those like them, these boys can be encouraged to model for classmates exactly what it means to treat others with kindness and compassion.

A windy day in February; a few boys will still try to play basketball outside at lunch recess. Keith is in the middle of it. He is the biggest boy in 5th grade. He also spends time in my pull-out group for high math ability. On this day, Keith is not playing basketball because of a broken thumb, but he is acting as coach. He is gathering boys around the baseline. So far there are only four, and now Keith is a recruiter. "Hey, do you want to play?" He has invited a boy to play who is close to the edge of behavior problems, and who has a full-time aid who shadows him all day. Soon, another boy has wandered up from the lower playground where he has had a conflict with some other kids. Keith is waving him over and trying to hurry him along. "Hey, we need another player. Why don't you play with us?"

This is what leadership looks like at age 11 and 12.

Can You Tell Me About Cancer?

One spring, I found myself with 18 newly identified gifted 2nd graders in my math and engineering group—mostly boys. I know most teachers would love just 18 kids in their class, but with *boy energy* and scissors, hot glue and craft saws, and little hands just learning how to work with all of these items, it was too much for me to handle. I had to warn the boys about the retractable metal measuring tape ("It's like a lightning bolt!") so many times that I eventually stored it away in a cabinet.

I split off a group of 5 boys into a different time slot—just "us guys." It was a diverse group—an athlete, an artist, quiet boys, boys full of psychomotor intensities, loud boys, and a couple boys somewhere on or near the spectrum. We shared three things in common, however: a love for "making stuff," giftedness, and a respect and friendly admiration for one of our group's members—Jalen. Jalen had been diagnosed that spring with leukemia.

It so happened that one of our group's meetings came just after a representative from Children's Hospital had come to Jalen's class to explain about leukemia.

As the boys came to my room for their GATE pull-out that day, one of them wanted to explain to me about leukemia. Others joined in, and soon they were all teaching me. Little experts. I listened and asked the boys clarifying questions. I was somewhat taken aback by their open-ness, and I worked hard to keep the conversation going. They were talking about important life issues, and I didn't want them to stop. As the boys explained to me details about cancer, their empathy was implied but clear.

Eventually, I told the boys how I felt about cancer, and then I asked them to tell me how other students in their class were feeling. Initially they talked about how others were feeling, but they soon started talking about how they, themselves, were feeling about cancer, too. Circumstances had backed us into the most important social-emotional lesson we would experience all year. Our most important social-emotional lessons, after all, come from life itself.

Circumstances had also aligned perfectly with how to talk to boys about feelings. In explaining about leukemia, the boys were not talking directly about feelings. Just like the best way to talk about emotional issues to boys is to allow them "to be doing other stuff" during the conversation or to be looking in another direction, teaching me about leukemia was a good way for the boys in my class to share thoughts and feelings without directly confronting them. They were doing other stuff and looking in another direction. It's wonderful the way they opened up—first talking about how others were feeling and then eventually feeling safe enough to talk about themselves. These boys had the choice of whether or not to share, and I have to think that me sharing my feelings contributed to the positive direction of the conversation.

Big Boys Don't Do That

Cole, a 4th grader, is using hot glue to place a dowel onto a portcullis prototype he is building. It is a delicate process, and his building skills don't quite match his engineering vision. As he places the dowel, the entire construction collapses, and Cole immediately begins to cry. "I'm not crying!" he exclaims—literally, to no one. Engrossed in their own projects, no other student has noticed what has taken place with Cole. He gasps down the tears and sits down, not knowing what to do next; but he has pleased the invisible judge and jury. His project fell apart, but he still feels like he won because he has been tough enough (almost) not to cry.

What if we dedicated some of our time in gifted and talented instruction to help gifted boys understand they are not alone? What if we used some of our time to help gifted boys understand that there are many ways of being tough? How about exploring topics like humility, patience, gratitude, compassion, and challenges? What if we helped them understand that the toughest boys are the boys who are tough enough to be kind and understanding? What if we helped boys understand that the toughest people still might cry in frustration?

How can we do these things, however, when most of our boys would strongly prefer anything but social-emotional lessons? We will be sneaky teachers…that's what we will do! We will make our lessons engaging and fun. We will meet these gifted boys on their own *boy* terms. We will understand that gifted boys may need help finding the proper language to discuss feelings. We will understand that they may not be willing to discuss feelings directly. We will therefore craft safe avenues of discourse and engaging methods. We will use humor and video and creativity and storytelling. We will construct and create and use metaphors. We will allow boys to perform improvisations and role play and pretend they are not themselves. We will encourage them to talk about what *other* boys—fictional boys—might do. We will encourage them to counsel fictional boys through difficult situations on the playground and at home. (See the *Doodles* social-emotional lesson at the end of this book.)

Except for this One...

One week, I had the opportunity to teach for 30 minutes in each 4th grade class in my building. Our academic goal was to understand central ideas in commercials by viewing and discussing the details together. But I had a dual purpose in mind, since I had a captive audience, and so I showed a commercial in which a big brother goes to great lengths to help his gravely ill sister. I engaged both boys and girls in a discussion about the boy in the commercial. One girl offered, "I wish that boy was my brother." I purposely solicited several opinions from boys—trying to choose ones who struggle with inappropriate behaviors on the playground. Even the roughest boys on the playground agreed that the boy in the commercial was not weak in any way. Instead, the consensus was that the boy was tough for not being afraid to show how much he loved his sister. Of course, the 4th grade boys admitted the boy in the commercial was tough. On the surface, we were just talking about the boy in the commercial, so despite their apparent emotional understanding, none of our boys had to feel direct ownership of the behavior.

In one 4th grade class, the discussion turned quite solemn. Each member of the class was attentive as several students began to share stories about compassion. A gifted boy—the boy with the greatest status and leadership potential in the 4th grade—volunteered a story about honoring someone he knew who had died. Ten seconds into the story, he could not continue. He buried his hands in his face so the others could not see him cry. Everyone knew what was happening, though. The class moved on—not drawing attention to him. At this age, boys can understand when another boy needs his space, and they respected their classmate. Never could I have demonstrated so strongly that there are many ways for a boy to be tough. Already a leader in his classroom and on the playground, this boy's position had only gained more respect. This is exactly how we hope our gifted boys—all boys—can be. These small moments add up and gain momentum between friends, in a classroom, and throughout a school. This is how boys can be tough in a healthy way.

References

Barker, Teresa, and Thompson, Michael (2009). *It's a Boy! Your Son's Development from Birth to Age 18*. New York: Ballantine Books.

Kerr, B. A., & Cohn, S. J. (2001). *Smart Boys: Talent, Manhood, and the Search for Meaning*. Scottsdale, AZ, US: Great Potential Press.

Kindlon, Dan, and Thompson, Michael (1999, 2000). *Raising Cain: Protecting the Emotional Life of Boys*. New York: Ballantine Books.

Lind, Sharon. (2011, September 14). *Overexcitability and the Gifted*. Retrieved from Sengifted.org.

Sword, Lesley K. (2011, September 14). *Emotional Intensity in Gifted Children*. Retrieved from Sengifted.org.

Chapter 4
Kids These Days

Previous versions of this chapter first appeared in the National Association for Gifted Children blog at NAGC.org. Search *Generation Z* to view the full list of articles.

Much of this chapter was written before the spring of 2020. Need I state the obvious, that life has changed, not only for school-aged children and young adults, but for everyone as well in these years that have followed? During the spring of 2020 and in the following school year, many students were required or chose to spend their school days online, and in the process we necessarily re-defined what was acceptable screen time. With students learning from home and in isolation from peers, our worries about social-emotional impacts grew. New information about the psychological consequences of using social media emerged—mostly negative consequences, and especially bad for young women. The social media platforms themselves are constantly in flux, as popularity bounces around like clothing trends. The political world of pre-2020 has shifted as well through Black Lives Matter, Me Too, the overturning of Roe vs. Wade, conspiracy theories, a Capitol insurrection, and the list goes on. Louder along with louder and angrier political and societal divisions will forever shift what our world looks like and how we live in it.

Generation Z kids, a couple years before I wrote these first drafts, comprised all of Kindergarten through 12th grade. Today, GenZ kids extend downward through only about half of the school system from 12th grades through 5th and 6th grades. By the time you read this book, the youngest from Generation Z may be in 8th grade, and the conversation will have already begun to shift to the next generation. Yet it's important to understand that a generation's label has no clear demarcation line. Each generation springs from those which came before and evolves, not in black and white societal data markers, but by degree. "Oh, you're a Millennial? Well…then you certainly can't possibly share any traits with Generation Z or Generation X, can you?" Of course you do.

What societal markers will Generation Alpha (2011-2025) bring—many of whom began Kindergarten and 1st grade rarely meeting their teachers face to face and rarely without a mask? One of my colleagues who teachers first grade said when the school mask mandate was lifted in our school district in 2022 that one of her students was surprised at how her teacher looked without a mask, that she looked like a different person. One of her other students assured, however, that her teacher looked the same from behind whether wearing a mask or not wearing a mask."

It remains to be seen how the pandemic and societal changes will shape our school children—our emerging Generation Alpha and our Generation Z kids. That's why I considered leaving this chapter out of this book. How could I begin to unpack the changes and influences from my first draft before the pandemic to publication? How could I possibly address all of these shifts in life and the way we live it? To leave this chapter out, however, would leave important discussions from previous drafts of this chapter inside my computer's trash bin. In the end, I decided the chapter still had important understandings to offer even though insights may shift and evolve. Gen Z will still be our school-aged kids for a long time to come. Already, however, they are our university and community college students as well, and they are entering—or have already entered—the world of work in full force. Many have already become parents themselves. When I work with teachers in professional development workshops, many of these teachers smiling back at me are the very Gen Z kids I'm teaching about.

Growing up Gifted and Generation Z: Safe Spaces

My colleague whispers, "We must be quieter than mice." It's astounding that 40 first and second graders can squeeze into this conference room between two classrooms, astounding that no one is poking someone else, trying to tickle somebody, fiddling with pencils or markers, or making animal noises. With the lights off in the small space—hardly more than a storage area—between my classroom and my colleague's 1st grade classroom, it's astounding that all 40 children are completely silent and gravely still. They all understand what is going on. We are in a *lock down, shelter-in-place* drill, and we will do this at least three more times before the end of the school year.

Generation Z has never known the world without internet. Generation Z has never known life without cell phones. As I write this, schools are planning post-pandemic maskless classrooms, or new COVID delta variant masking requirements, and trying to figure out logical rules for quarantines in a partly vaccinated system: Gen Z students have yet to experience school life without *the huddles, lock-downs, and sheltering-in-place.*

When I first started teaching, a *lock-in* was what students called a fun all-night sleepover at the school; but *lock-ins* are now threats and precautions in a school's neighborhood to be shared on social media and even on "crawl line"' on local news stations. Though I grew up with the vague threat of nuclear war lurking in the background, today's kids see their fears come true, broadcast in the media, with masks and plexiglass barriers as a constant reminder that health and safety cannot be taken for granted. For gifted kids who tend to be more idealistic and more sensitive than other kids—who are sometimes plagued by existential questions other children do not ponder—this daily dose of our more alarming reality has the potential to spawn enormous anxiety.

Grounded in a real potential danger, the safety drills are, nonetheless, also part of a larger trend of safety in general for GenZ kids—a trend that started a generation or more before 2020. Safety now demands playgrounds with six-inch-deep beds of wood chips, carpeted gym floors, youth league baseball pitchers wearing chest protectors, strapping into car seats until past kindergarten, being picked up or dropped off at school or walking to school only with a parent escort, bike helmets, ski helmets, skateboard helmets, wrist guards, shin guards, goggles and water wings. This generation understands safety to the extent that even perceived emotional threats are not tolerated. College campuses have begun to set aside "emotional safe spaces" where students are protected from words or ideas they find disturbing. How deep, one wonders, does the anxiety over safety extend past masks, plexiglass barriers around school desks, and the huddle?

Where does the emphasis on safety, both emotional and physical, leave the gifted learner who feels life more intensely, makes complex connections, perceives more nuanced levels and subtleties, and is touched deeply by the experiences of others? Where does this leave our overthinkers, our kids who imagine and re-imagine their ideal selves and their ideal world? With life's realities on electronic devices at this generation's fingertips like never before, where does this leave gifted learners who want to save the world but are faced with the existential possibility that they may live in a world that could be precariously tipped beyond saving?

As parents and teachers, it makes sense that we want to provide safe spaces for our children who are always just a smartphone finger-swipe away from learning about the next tragedy, the next act of gun violence reviewed and replayed in a 24 hour news cycle, the next climate catastrophe, the next warning about the next COVID variation. A couple of years ago, the parents of a friend decided it would not be fair to tell their gifted autistic daughter that a beloved great aunt had passed away. They felt it would be too much to handle, that she would agonize over the news, be distraught, be inconsolable. They thought that by keeping the sad news from her, they could protect her presumably delicate emotions. What will happen, though, at the next family gathering without the beloved aunt? Will their daughter simply forget the aunt ever existed? Will she never question why her great aunt seems to have disappeared? Instead of building shelters, we should caringly expose young adults to uncomfortable discourse, just as we must have them endure *lock-downs, shelters-in-place* and safety drills. This is important because learning to process the reality of uncomfortable and challenging situations is a healthy step toward developing the skills of understanding, acceptance, critical thinking, and maturity. We should maintain a facilitated discourse about the issues which surround us. Our gifted children are full of emotional and intellectual intensities, but they also have a vast capacity for critical thinking, creativity, and problem-solving.

Huddled together in the shared breakout room between two classrooms, we wait for the announcement containing the code word which tells us all is clear and the drill is over. I wonder about Theo—a brilliant little mathematician whose emotions might swing rapidly from zero to eleven. I wonder about Samantha, our 1st grade poet, who happily announced to me one day as students gathered their backpacks and coats to go home, "I love this part of the day because it means I get to go home and be with my family." I wonder about Grayson, whose tags are too scratchy inside his shirt and have to be removed, and who comes to my desk with his nose tucked inside his shirt when I have coffee because the smell "just gets to him." Even 5 or 10 minutes in a huddle in the dark is going to challenge his sensitivities. I wonder about Shelby, who I witnessed carefully closing a book on her desktop and staring ahead solemnly for so long that I had to ask her if something was the matter: "That was the most incredible book I have ever read," was her whispered response.

Their hearts are full. Their world is full of beauty and tragedy alike. As neurologically diverse individuals, they carry creativity, imagination and a spirit of wonder. But with these powerful life tools comes the potential for not only brilliance, but also devastating disappointment. I worry because I understand how deeply they feel. I worry because, despite our best intentions, we cannot protect them forever. In the process of educating our children, I believe we as teachers and parents can both protect and guide, nurture and soothe. Generation Z thinks globally, is stunningly accepting of differences, and carries vast potential, but they must be cautiously, deliberately and wisely encouraged to emerge from their safe spaces to truly make a difference.

References

Daniels, Susan, and Piechowski, Michael. *Living with Intensities*. Great Potential Press. 2009.

Haidt, Jonathan, and Lukianoff, Greg. *The Coddling of the American Mind* on the Atlantic website: (https://www.theatlantic.com/magazine/archive/2015/09/the-coddling-of-the-american-mind/399356/) accessed 12/14/19.

Twenge, Jean M., Ph.D. *iGen: Why Today's Super-Connected Kids are Growing Up Less Rebellious, More Tolerant, Less Happy—and Completely Unprepared for Adulthood*. Atria: 2017.

6 Reasons Why Intelligent People Fail to be Happy. Learning Mind website (https://www.learning-mind.com/fail-to-be-happy-intelligent/) accessed 11/26/19.

Growing up Gifted and Generation Z: A Problem with Compassion?

One of my favorite professional development sessions to teach is an introduction to gifted learners and giftedness. During the first session, teachers respond "true" or "false" to statements based on some of the prevailing myths of giftedness. Teachers typically do pretty well with the list. A gifted learner will be talented in everything they put their mind to…false. Gifted learners are always the best students…false. One statement, however, consistently trips them up: Gifted kids are less empathic than other kids. Many teachers believe that myth to be true. I don't know what fosters a belief in this myth. Do the teachers assume elitist attitudes and privilege are internalized by gifted kids, making them less empathic and compassionate? Do they believe gifted kids to be bullies when, often, the reverse is true? Have they had negative experiences with gifted students when they were school children themselves or as teachers in their own classrooms?

We older generations are sometimes also fond of wagging our fingers in disapproval at younger generations. "Kids these days don't care. Kids these days hide behind screens and don't build relationships. They don't build empathy and connections the way we used to." This combination between a belief that gifted kids are less empathic and unfair generational judgements concerns me.

Casting Understanding Instead of Throwing Stones

Generation Z gifted kids are not less compassionate. Kids these days think globally. Their digital connectivity brings with it the opportunity to share perspectives and develop understanding about others around the world like never before—an incredible potential to want what's right and to do right backed by the gifted individual's keen sense of justice. Before we start wagging our fingers at an entire generation or propagating myths about giftedness, let's remember that Generation Z is the generation of:

- Greta Thunberg, the teenage climate activist named *Time Magazine's* Person of the Year for 2019

- The Parkland teens—also named *Time Magazine's* Persons of the Year—whose passion set in motion *Enough: March for Our Lives*—the largest youth protest since the Vietnam War, with 88 sister events and an estimated 1.2 to 2 million participants
- Leaders in the Black Lives Matter movement working to "bring justice, healing, and freedom to Black people across the globe"—many of whom are my former students, now in their early to mid-twenties, posting several times a day on social media and attending local rallies at the height of the movement. My own gifted daughter stood with two friends holding a sign one afternoon in a small fishing village in Alaska where she lives, a Generation Z demonstration of three.

A Problem with Compassion

One of the psychological challenges these past few years has been anticipatory grief—the fear that the worst is about to happen. Generation Z—the generation of emotional and physical safety—has been surrounded by COVID and gun violence, assaulting their feelings of safety. These past few years have been particularly difficult for teachers and students alike.

According to grief expert David Kessler, anticipatory grief is an uncertainty about the future that usually centers around death. During these past few years, the anticipatory grief wasn't necessarily about an uncertainty surrounding death, but rather fear for the loss of safety in one's life. As restrictions were lifted in schools, each day wearing a mask to school brought a reminder of the uncertainty for students. COVID could never be locked out entirely, and neither could gun violence. The school shooting in Uvalde demonstrated to us that unlocked doors, in fact, might bring an even more frightening consequence than COVID.

In uncertain times, anticipatory grief can easily lead to anxiety as our minds race to unsettling images about what might be. I and all of my teaching colleagues have imagined and re-imagined exactly what we would do if faced with our own Columbine, Parkland, or Uvalde. For gifted GenZers who are highly visual, possess active imaginations, and deep, intense emotions, these imagined scenarios can be frighteningly vivid. Added to that are the anxious feelings of existential dread, feelings of grief over the meaninglessness of life, death, and loneliness which gifted children often develop at a young age. Our gifted children make connections that others to do not make, absorb life (including the pain and negative emotions of others) with uncommon clarity, and get swept away in such large, emotional imaginations. One road takes our children toward anticipatory grief and anxiety. Another road leads to images of calamity inside a classroom. Existential dread waits at the end of the road. At these intersections, though, lie empathy and its actionable counterpart, compassion.

An ironic follow up for the incorrect response to the myth that gifted children are less compassionate than others is that they may actually be too compassionate. But aren't empathy and compassion good things? Dr. Nicole A. Tetreault answers that question directly, "Too much empathy can be a disadvantage because it can hinder one's processing of other information." For children and young adults who can be intensely focused, these feelings of empathy and compassion run the risk of becoming unbearable.

But Shouldn't We Be Doing Something?

Many of our gifted children may be feeling an existential urgency that there is something very important they should be doing—that time is running out, but we are just sitting and waiting. Shouldn't we be doing something? We can help empower our kids in small and appropriate ways. In her book *When Your Child Goes Overboard: Fears and Compassionate Concerns*, Nancy Robinson, Ph.D. explains to parents that feelings should be both experienced and acknowledged. Feelings are genuine, but we should help our children avoid being overwhelmed by modelling calm and inviting open dialogues about fears.

Many world events can trigger an existential dive, and we parents and educators might be wondering what is too much news, or what news might not be appropriate. In their podcast, *What to Say to Your Kids When the News Gets Scary*, Anya Kamenetz and Cory Turner advise parents to limit a child's exposure to 'breaking' news. Within this new cultural dynamic of a constant news cycle, some have made it a habit to simply leave the television tuned to news channels during the day—forgetting that scary news might break as one goes about one's daily business. For the bigger stories, it's important to ask children what they've heard and how they are feeling. Kamenetz, for example, remembers hearing about guerilla warfare in Bosnia when she was a child. She remembers seeing images of tanks in the streets. Not having a sense of geography, she feared that tanks would appear on her street too. Misunderstanding the terminology, she feared that gorillas were engaged in acts of war against humans. It's important for adults to provide both factual information as well as perspective and context, avoiding vague labels like "bad guys" which might imprint deeply in young, compassionate souls. When tragedy strikes, the podcasters go on to say, "…look for the helpers and concentrate on the helpers; then volunteer to go out into your own community and help as well. Take action through compassion."

Empathy involves taking action guided by one's compassion. Empathy researcher Daniel Goleman states, "Not only do we want students to feel and acknowledge empathy toward others, we also want them to apply their problem-solving and critical thinking skills to positively impact situations that are causing distress for others (as cited in *Developing Compassionate Empathy in Gifted Children*). Even in their youth, gifted learners are uniquely prepared to do this. Resources are already out there and easily accessible. The National Society for Gifted and Talented offers 'tween' and teen courses that provide structure in developing compassionate empathy. The Making Caring Common Project from the Harvard Graduate School of Education is another excellent resource for gifted students, available through links on the National Association for Gifted Children's website, in which compassionate children are linked with service organizations and community leaders who are actively involved in bringing compassion and empathy to community involvement. NAGC has also developed resources and tip sheets focused on social-emotional support for gifted children in this unique time.

With Compassion We Move Forward Together

Step back with me to late spring, 2021, more than a year into the pandemic. The trajectory of my school district has been similar to many others: periods of lockdowns, periods of virtual learning, periods of in-person classes involving social-distancing and plexiglass barriers, and many cancellations of activities—school icons like sports and other school functions that are hallmarks and signposts of a school year passing. We missed the Halloween parade. We missed the fall carnival. We played our basketball and volleyball seasons in masks. We missed exchanging school pictures. We missed school dances. We missed field day. We missed in-person graduation.

On a playground before school on this spring day in 2021, our bodies are stretched into twenty feet tall shadows as the sun rises behind us. We all wear masks for today's modified pandemic schedule, and many of us pause to watch a second grader twirl and dance. She is watching her shadow as it moves fluidly on the playground blacktop in front of her, and even in a mask, we can see how she concentrates on making her shadow move "just so." Other kids notice and begin dancing with their shadows, too—forming an uneven line of seven or eight children dancing with their shadows. Outside a school, still inside a pandemic in 2021, these children inherently understand these moments of hope.

Grief expert David Kessler advises us to "stock up on compassion," as those around us are sure to experience grief at different levels and in different ways. I believe our gifted kids have already got that covered because the lives of gifted children are different from others. They are built with an intensity of feeling and desire to act inspired by compassion. Dr. Evan Brockman shared a story of a profoundly gifted girl at the SENG national conference (7/23/21) who realized she was different from others as a first grader. One day this girl decided it was her duty to make sure the teacher understood what all of the other children in the class were feeling: "I was responsible for the whole class," the first grader explained, "which kept me busy making sure others were always OK. If someone in the class wasn't doing okay, it was my fault because I wasn't doing my job right." Another first grader in another year—this time in my literacy group—was asked to explain in a drawing how it might feel to fly. While most students responded by drawing pictures showing the thrill and exhilaration of flight, Rachel drew herself with a frown, her arms waving as if she were about to fall out of the sky. She was looking down on her home, outside of which sat her wheelchair-bound little sister, and the caption for her drawing said, "I am sad because I want to go home. I miss my family." Yes, our gifted kids have it covered—this compassion question.

GenZ gifted kids will be O.K. There may be no better generation to move us forward with their global views and their acceptance of a person's right to be who they are, to express their individuality. The youngest members of Generation Z will take present feelings forward—not necessarily the specifics, but the prevailing feelings of the time. These past couple years they have vividly felt a world re-setting its priorities of love and family and taking stock about what is important in life. These youngest members of Generation Z have the compassion we will depend on in our future.

References

Berinato, Scott. March, 23, 2020. That discomfort you're feeling is grief. *Harvard Business Review* online https://hbr.org/2020/03/that-discomfort-youre-feeling-is-grief

Cheema, Amal. March 29, 2020. An appeal to youth to face Coronavirus with self-sacrifice, not selfishness. Capradio online at https://www.capradio.org/news/npr/story?storyid=822642383

Kamenetz, Anya, and Turner, Cory. 2020. What to say to your kids when the news gets scary. NPR. Accessed online at https://www.npr.org/2019/04/24/716704917/when-the-news-is-scary-what-to-say-to-kids

Robinson, Nancy M. 2014. When your child goes overboard: Fears and compassionate concerns. SENG Library. Accessed online at https://www.sengifted.org/post/when-your-child-goes-overboard-fears-and-compassionate-concerns

Swicord, Barbara. 2019. Developing compassionate empathy in gifted children. Giftedstudy.org.

Tetrault, Nicole A. 2017. Emotionally gifted and navigating the world. SENG Library. Accessed online at https://www.sengifted.org/post/emotionally-gifted-and-navigating-the-world#:~:text=%20Emotionally%20gifted%20and%20navigating%20the%20world%20,why.%20.%20Allowing%20the%20individual%20to...%20More%20

Growing up Gifted and Generation Z: Bomb Cyclone Perfectionism

At 10:00 a.m. on a school day in March, I wonder if the school district has made a mistake calling for a snow day. It is gray, calm and nearly 50 degrees. Except for strange looking wispy clouds, it could be any other spring day. Were all the weather predictions wrong? No: 30 minutes later, I cannot see the street in front of my house through horizontal snow, and the bomb cyclone had come as predicted. The first blast of its wind had sounded like someone pounding on our front door. Neighbors were still clearing their property of downed trees and limbs well into the summer months. From a little grey to stormy winds in just minutes: I've seen this in my students many times. With generational anxiety in youth at an all-time high, feelings of inadequacy pushing toward the distress level, rejections only a smartphone swipe away, and gifted kids wrapped inside feelings more intensely than others, Generation Z gifted kids wait inside an atmosphere that has the potential for bomb cyclone perfectionism.

In her chapter about perfectionism in *Living with Intensities,* Linda Silverman cites two research studies that show approximately 1/4th of gifted sixth graders are dysfunctional perfectionists—not neurotically dysfunctional, but conscientiously dysfunctional. Anecdotally as parents, teachers, and counsellors of gifted children, however, we are all too familiar with perfectionist responses. Even if the association between cognitive ability and perfectionism is inconclusive as cited in a 2020 study (Lavrijsen, et al), the interplay of perfectionism and intensity of experience in gifted individuals is of true concern. Conscientious perfectionists are keenly aware of their potential, critical of their own performances across a broad spectrum of tasks both large and small, expect success, and want to shine—not just for themselves—but also for those they love and respect. Because school has come so easily, praise has been given so expectedly, and challenges have been so rare for gifted individuals, an almost effortless perfection has become a regular part of our gifted kids' days. As years pass and life and school become more complicated, this chase for perfection might sigh momentarily with satisfaction, but often waylays its racers in a cycle of feelings of shame and inadequacy. How might these perfectionist tendencies play out for our current Generation Z students?

> "[Bombogenesis] can happen when a cold air mass collides with a warm air mass...when a storm's barometric pressure drops by 24 millibars...in 24 hours."
> —National Oceanic and Atmospheric Administration NOAA

According to data collected in the *Monitoring the Future Surveys* (1989-2015), 37% of teenagers are 'neutral', 'mostly agree', or 'agree' with the statement that "I can't do anything right." This is an 11% increase from the millennial low of 26% in 1992. For perfectionists who play out an increasing portion of their lives online and in social media (high school seniors spend twice as much time online each day as compared to 2005) this trend is especially concerning.

Platforms such as Instagram and Facebook trigger social validation loops—re-wiring one's brain in search of continuing validation. For both self-oriented perfectionists who engage in strict self-evaluation and for socially prescribed perfectionists who seek others' validation, the virtual *thumbs up*, *hearts*, and *likes* potentially add one more layer to a protective, perfectionist cloak. Consider the perfectionist posting a small victory on social media, absorbing the validation of *likes* and positive comments, checking back to see the number growing. "Will this be a record for me?" Now consider this same perfectionist with a future post which does not receive the same number of positive responses (oh, and these gifted minds can certainly store data for comparison!). "I guess they don't like me as much as they used to. Other people get more responses than I do. I never deserved it anyway." Those fears in mind, now it becomes paramount that the social-media stage is carefully set and orchestrated to show only the most wonderful version of oneself. After all, look at all the wonderful lives and experiences one sees each time one scrolls down the page.

But is it the real and authentic version of oneself that other people suddenly don't like so much? Not likely. Is a perfectionist apt to post a failure, an inadequacy, a slight, or an embarrassment? They are not, but such behavior would actually be one of the healthiest self-assessments a perfectionist could venture into, along with forming and maintaining healthy, true connections and friendships. But in a generation which is less likely to engage in face-to-face interactions than any other, opportunities to show one's authentic self in person are diminished. As Brené Brown says in her book, *The Gifts of Imperfection*, "If you've worked so hard to make everything look just right, the stakes are high when it comes to your authentic self." Not getting a *like* on an orchestrated social media post is one thing, but what happens when you believe no one likes your authentic self?

> "As the air rises, wind spirals in at the base of the storm. All bomb cyclones are not hurricanes. But sometimes, they can take on characteristics that make them look like hurricanes...Much of the danger lies in the fact that bomb cyclones can take people by surprise."—Daniel Swan, as quoted by NBC News, 10/18/19"

We GenX and Millennial parents look out for our kids like no other generation has before us. With smaller families than in past generations, parents spend more time nurturing each child. Generation Z is growing up more slowly, more protected by the adults in their lives. Adolescence is extended. Data trends show that activities like getting a driver's license, drinking alcohol, having sex, and attending unchaperoned parties have been postponed, in some cases until college. *Adulting* is a new social media meme. Self-deprecating humor through videos and commercials pokes fun at Millennial and GenZers alike—with twenty and thirty somethings congratulating themselves for doing laundry, cooking, paying bills, and shopping for groceries. We have grown up now. Look what we can do!

We parents are vigilant and protective. It's understandable. We hope our children will be happy and enjoy experiences we may have missed, so if we have the means to make those experiences possible, we sign up. We sign our children up for engineering camps and private music lessons and competitive sports leagues. We want our children to do well, achieve, earn scholarships which will help pay for huge tuition expenses. Many of us might foster perfectionist behavior without meaning to—even with an understanding of the pitfalls of perfectionism at work in ourselves. Encouraging achievement, checking homework folders and helping our children pursue passions through after school programs or in athletics, guiding our kids to leadership or public service opportunities which build their scholarship portfolios will likely train our children to tie their self-concepts to their performances in and out of the classroom, despite our hopes that they develop an intrinsic to value learning and growth independent of accomplishments.

Twenge reports that GenZers have come to value extrinsic rewards more highly than previous generations. Satisfaction with school—as expressed by 12th grade surveys—is lower than ever. A 4.0 grade point average seems almost low. It used to be *perfect*. Now how high can a student's GPA reach with AP and honors classes? 4.5? 5.0? Add to this that an increased generational external locus of control, and the result correlates with anxiety and depression. The winds begin to spiral ominously.

WGBH's stories on the pressure to succeed show us where perfectionism can attach itself even before kindergarten. One parent spoke about how, at five months pregnant, she and her husband sought what they thought would be a high-quality daycare, only to be laughed at for their tardiness in applying. Clinical psychologist David Gleason states, "Increasingly, affluent students are over-protected, over-scheduled and overwhelmed before they have the capacity to manage stress. The parents who are now old enough to have children are themselves products of this very system, so they don't know anything else." The findings of Lavrijsen, et al, support this notion—citing high parental expectations and parental criticism as a positive correlation with high achieving students' worrying excessively over mistakes.

> "But while any given storm may not turn out to be as apocalyptic as the term *bomb cyclone* would suggest, you should still take extreme care during any major weather event. Ideally, no one will freak out at all. But you should absolutely keep an eye on your local forecasts to know how much you need to prepare."
> —Rachel Feltman for Popular Science, *What the Heck is a Bomb Cyclone?*

Linda Silverman reminds us that healthier, self-oriented perfectionists had parents who did not communicate perfection;

rather, these parents expressed unconditional love and support. Perfectionism and wanting to do well are two different things. Wanting to do well is good if we reframe mistakes as learning experiences. Wanting to do well means risk-making and realizing nothing is mastered without practice. Wanting to do well is healthy growth. Perfectionism is not.

Even as the skies turn grey, there are ways to encourage safety amidst increasing winds and swirling clouds. In *iGen*, Twenge offers tips for Generation Z employers, and some of this advice reads as best practices in guiding perfectionists. Growing up slowly, GenZ needs more frequent guidance and reassurance, and as this is a generation eager to do well despite fears of failure, GenZ students will tend to respond well to support. This is a generation that wants to feel safe both physically and emotionally, and perfectionists insulate themselves for emotional safety. We've heard it before when trying to advise or direct or correct one: "I got it! I know! I heard you! Would you please just stop talking about it!" As parents and mentors, we need to keep feedback more frequent, brief and direct, without coddling. That doesn't mean, however, that we shouldn't express care and support. In a world of virtual friendships, in-person relationships are still of high value—maybe even more so. Let's approach those we love (and ourselves while we're at it) by always letting them know we are on their side and that it's safe to be less than perfect. As Twenge states, "Specifically say *I want you to succeed*."

This is a generation loaded with talent, a generation who—like all others before it—is finding its place in its own way amidst its own challenges: immersion in online media, unhealthy and seemingly immovable divisions in ideologies, a changing climate and the true fears that go along with it. This generation's oldest members are becoming parents and teachers themselves. A young colleague and gifted girl, a middle school teacher with many gifted kids now in her own classroom, recently told me, "I feel overwhelmed every day by both the possibilities of these kids and the speed of life around them. We start each day in my class by simply *being*—heads down on our desks with the lights off just like I used to do after lunch when I was in first grade. More than one student has told me this is the best part of their school day. Kids need these mindful moments just to re-group."

Let's remember there is pain in perfectionism. Perfectionism is not something to be laughed off or shrugged off or spoken about as if it were an immature behavior one will outgrow. There are true consequences for unhealthy perfectionists. Playing it safe, wrapping oneself in insulated blankets, and hiding one's true and vulnerable self not only limit our achievement but also limit our potential for growth and relationships as well. Perhaps all of us—parents and children alike—should start being kinder to ourselves. Perhaps we all need heads-down-lights-off-mindful moments in the middle of each day. And I say *we* and *us* and *ourselves* quite purposefully, because so often behind a perfectionist stands another. As Breneé Brown so poignantly states, "It is clear we cannot give our children what we do not have."

References

Brown, Breneé. *The Gift of Imperfection: Let Go of Who You Think You're Supposed to Be, and Embrace Who You Are*. Hazelden Publishing: 2010.

Carapezza, Kirk. *The College Pressure Cooker: High Achieving Students, High Mental Health Risks* WGBH website (https://www.wgbh.org/news/education/2019/11/19/the-college-pressure-cooker-high-achieving-students-high-mental-health-risks) accessed 11/26/19.

Carapezza, Kirk. *The Pressures on Kids—They're Born into It*. WGBH website (https://www.wgbh.org/news/education/2019/11/18/the-pressures-on-kids-theyre-born-into-it) accessed 11/26/19.

Daniels, Susan, and Piechowski Michael, Eds. *Living with Intensity.* Great Potential Press: 2009.

Gray, Peter, Ph.D. *The Decline of Play and Rise in Children's Mental Disorders*. Psychology Today website (https://www.psychologytoday.com/us/blog/freedom-learn/201001/the-decline-play-and-rise-in-childrens-mental-disorders) accessed 11/11/19.

Lavrijsen, Jeroen. Soenens, Bart. Vansteenkiste, Karine Vershcueren. 2020. Is intelligence related to perfectionism? Multidimensional perfectionism and parent antecedents among adolescents across varying levels of cognitive ability. *Journal of Psychology*. Accessed online at https://onlinelibrary.wiley.com/doi/abs/10.1111/jopy.12606

Pychyl, Timothy, Ph.D. *What Flavor of Perfectionist are You? It Matters!* Psychology Today website (https://www.psychologytoday.com/us/blog/dont-delay/200804/what-flavor-perfectionist-are-you-it-matters) accessed 11/11/19.

Tetrault, Nicole, Ph.D. *Our Brains on Smarphones, (Un)social Media, and Our Mental Health.* (https://www.nicoletetreault.com/single-post/2018/03/07/Our-brains-on-smartphones-unsocial-media-and-our-mental-health) accessed 11/15/19.

Twenge, Jean M., Ph.D. *iGen: Why Today's Super-Connected Kids are Growing Up Less Rebellious, More Tolerant, Less Happy—and Completely Unprepared for Adulthood.* Atria: 2017.

Webb, James T., Ph.D., et al. *A Parent's Guide to Gifted Children*. Great Potential Press: 2007.

Growing Up Gifted and Generation Z: Vision for Equity

My son once announced to me that he had read four books in one week. "Well, actually," he clarified, "if you want to get technical about it, I didn't *read* the books. I *listened* to them as audiobooks or watched them on YouTube." This made perfect sense to me. After all, this is the kid who spent hours building a website and a whole week of evenings creating a video for a high school English project. But he had never really acquired the knack of immersing himself in pages full of words. At 23 years old, he is one of the older Generation Z gifted kids, and like many GenZ gifted kids, my son typically satisfies his intellectual intensities not necessarily outside of, but parallel to, the written word.

As a former Language Arts teacher, I sometimes find myself thinking of reading as the sacred key to knowledge and understanding. Undoubtedly one of the most powerful and wonderful processes in education is a first grader walking into a classroom in August as a non-reader and walking out of the same classroom in May as a reader, their intellectual world having been changed forever. Many of us were drawn to teaching because we loved school, and loving school often meant loving books. We are at home in elementary schools where up to 80% of instruction is language-based. Words are a large part of who we are, but this is not so true for most of the kids we teach.

Data from 2015 (Twenge, p. 51) shows that Generation Z seniors spent over two hours texting, two hours on the internet, one and one-half hours electronic gaming, and half an hour on video chat each day. In 2015, teens were spending twice as much time online as seniors a decade before. Put another way, that's six and one-half hours each day not reading books. 60% of all GenZ kids cite YouTube as their preferred way to learn, and in recent years, my gifted elementary students have begun listing *professional gamer* and *YouTuber* as future career choices—though, as one of my second graders pointed out—"My dad says that's not really a valid career choice."

I have news for you, Dad. You are living in the past, my friend.

Still Love a Story

This is not to say our GenZ kids disdain words. My students love storytelling and sharing picture books and reading aloud in *circle time* just as much as kids always have—maybe even more. Recent research published in the *Journal of Neuroscience* explained that listening to audiobooks and reading paper books showed virtually identical brain activity. This is not to say that reading in and of itself does not have inherent intellectual and academic value. But we understand that intelligence, learning, student engagement, achievement and discovery go well beyond the written word. Let's step back and survey the education landscape in our present cultural context and recognize that the one of the keys to student engagement for Generation Z is visual and nonverbal.

Our cultural landscape shows an incredibly visual experience for our students: Twitter, TikTok, YouTube, Snapchat, Instagram, Video Games, Netflix, Hulu, emoticons which claim to express every nuance of every mood we can think of, visual memes that gain traction and go viral; and the evolution of these distractions is much faster than one generation. If you are listening to your Bluetooth earphones now, even your texts will be read aloud to you. And there's no need for writing these texts, either, as the voice to text options have become quite effective. Undoubtedly, screen time poses many concerns, but at the same time, what we see and process visually—our brain's visual-spatial sketchpad—is essential for learning. Working memory operates through two channels: sounds (or phonological loops), and the visual-spatial "sketchpad." This working memory is a greater predictor of school-based success at age 5 than reading scores, motivation, a positive attitude, math scores, and IQ (says Eric Jensen, Ph.D., as presented at the Colorado Symposium 6/29/18). There is, in short, a vast potential for all children in what they process by combining pictures and words. Have you noticed how visual and rich in graphics publications such as *Time* and *USA Today* have become? Part of their appeal is that we don't just want to *read* these publications. We want to *see* them too, and these publications are perfect examples of the powerful imprinting process of working memory.

One measurement of Gen Z students' vast visual potential is through nonverbal ability tests—emphasis on the word *potential.*

As educators of gifted learners, we strive to honor all abilities and broad spectrums of talent in all cultures—to not leave anyone out. This is our vision for equity.

For 39 free mini-lessons for critical thinking using short videos, visit www.giftedlearners.org and click "KIDVIDTHINK DAILY."

One Pathway for Gifted Equity

Donna Ford— our nation's leading voice for gifted equity—cites nonverbal ability tests as her "first choice" for both culturally-linguistically diverse learners as well as for African-Americans (Beyond Giftedness Conference. Arvada, Colorado, 2/28/2020). Two widely respected state guides, Iowa's *Identifying Gifted and Talented English Language Learners* and Missouri's *Identifying and Serving Traditionally Underrepresented Gifted Students*, encourage using nonverbal ability tests in the gifted identification process. In Colorado, the state's largest (and very diverse) Denver Public Schools has turned to the Naglieri Test of Nonverbal Ability (NNAT) as its universal screening instrument. Denver, and nearby Colorado Springs, are the two most diverse school districts in Colorado, and both use the nonverbal testing (along with multiple measures) from the Cognitive Abilities Test (CogAT) to identify students for gifted programs. Even though a meta-analysis (Lee, et al.) found that nonverbal ability tests may not be as good at identifying gifted children of color as once believed, identification results were still better in comparison with traditional methods of identification. Nonverbal ability is a more effective avenue to recognize and develop potential, not only for culturally-linguistically diverse learners, African-American students and other underrepresented populations like twice-exceptional learners, but for an entire generation of students with visual orientations.

High nonverbal ability scores are shared by architects, engineers, choreographers, quarterbacks and coaches, artists, graphic designers, film directors, designers in every field, electricians, Pulitzer Prize winning photographers, mechanics, surgeons, and Einstein himself, who said, "My thoughts did not come in any verbal formulation. I rarely think in words at all." Poetry is not exclusive to words, and poets might also work in nonverbal mediums. Any time a person seeks to arrange, connect, construct, envision, design, pattern, or choreograph, they rely on nonverbal ability to do so. But nonverbal ability is not mutually exclusive of or counter to verbal ability. Think of *Time Magazine*, think of your favorite movie, and think of the best advertising campaigns which rely on a memorable combination of images and words. Verbal communication, itself, is much more than words. Human communication is up to 3/4^{ths} nonverbal and includes gestures, posture, movement, and facial expressions as well as the words themselves—a combination of nuances our brain's powerful visual processing and language centers use for us to react and understand.

Who are the students who score high on nonverbal ability tests? They are students like Kayla, born in the Philippines and still learning English at my school when I met her as a 2nd grader. She was full of curiosity—an inventor, a designer, and an artist. By 5th grade she had begun to score high enough on a standardized achievement tests to qualify for gifted services, yet she had already stood out in the gifted program for three years. They are students like Rachel and Hannah Begay—twin sisters of Native American heritage—poetic and artistic and accomplished writers even though their strongest ability scores were nonverbal. They are the dozen or more boys over the years in my gifted program (usually boys but sometimes girls) who have 30 to 40 point gaps between their verbal and non-verbal ability scores. Often emotionally intense, they almost franticly consume wooden dowels, craft sticks, hot glue, and cardboard. At the end of the session, they sprint out of my room lest I might ask them to write something.

They are students like Becca, a 4th grader who scored in the 97th percentile on the Naglieri Test of Nonverbal Ability, yet was also attending remediation sessions for reading. On her student profile, her mother had written, "She loves scarves. She loves the different shapes, the different colors and patterns, and the different styles. Her closet is full of scarves! She delights in finding combinations in colors with different outfits and the look and feel of the materials." I don't doubt that someday we may be wearing *Becca Originals*. They are students like a twice-exceptional student who had solved every puzzle in my classroom electronics kit by the end of the first quarter, and the girl who scored in the 65th percentile in reading yet won the class spelling bee ("I can just see the words in my head."). And they are students like Jason, a 4th grader who had turned his spelling test into a work of graphic art out of frustration. He graduated college with a double major in computer engineering and physics and now manages projects in Silicon Valley. If it weren't for nonverbal ability testing, none of these students would have been included in gifted programming.

We Missed Everything?

Professor C. Own Lo asks, "What if Mozart lived in Mongolia?" What if Mozart did not live in a culture that afforded the opportunity to showcase his amazing musical abilities? What if someone in 2020, however, was amazing at designing and creating and constructing, yet rarely got that opportunity in school? What if an African-American boy in 2020 possessed verve and storytelling abilities that were a delight to anyone who witnessed them outside of a school building, but inside that school building, the same boy was seen as "hyperactive" or disrespectful or an unwilling writer? What if a student literally did not have the words yet—not in English? As gifted educators, we understand that a part of gifted identification is creating opportunities and resources so that students with a broad range of strong abilities may engage wholeheartedly and creatively to express their giftedness.

Meet Jordy and Shay. They're 3rd graders in my STEM talent pool—having scored between the 90th and the 94th percentile on the CogAT nonverbal battery test. They had to miss the very first session of the talent pool because they had been double-booked in reading remediation at the same time.

"When you have finished with reading group, come down to my classroom. I will help you get started and catch up on the project," I promised.

Finally arriving when the other students were just leaving, Jordy was in tears. "We missed everything?"

Yes, they did on that day, but I wouldn't allow that to happen again. We got a little more creative with scheduling because yes, absolutely Jordy and Shay needed individual attention in reading…but yes, absolutely Jordy and Shay needed individual attention for their nonverbal abilities. And, by the way, both typically outshined the brightest students in my talent pool in their STEM constructions—especially in the more creative projects.

Interested in one of those STEAM activities from my group? For a free STEAM activity for upper elementary gifted—Make Your Own Tops—visit: https://www.teacherspayteachers.com/Product/STEAM-Activity-Make-Your-Own-TOPS-Upper-Elementary-and-Gifted-and-Talented-3179287

The most beautiful and compelling trait common to Generation Z is their acceptance of others. As Dr. Jean M. Twenge phrases it on the last page her book *iGen*, "They're exquisitely tolerant and have brought a new awareness of equality" (p. 313). We already understand that we can't define giftedness solely through achievement. Let's invite students who show potential into our gifted classes and talent pools and let these students grow their academic talent through challenging, engaging, creative and diverse activities. Let's serve students first, and identify giftedness second. As educators, we celebrate children. It is more than our charge. It is who we are. It's why we became teachers in the first place.

References

Genota, Lauraine. 2018. Generation z prefers learning from YouTube, not books. *Education Week*. Accessed online: https://www.edweek.org/technology/generation-z-prefers-learning-from-youtube-not-books/2018/08

Lee, Hueseong, et al. 2021. A meta-analytic evaluation of Naglieri Nonverbal Ability Test: Exploring its validity evidence and effectiveness in equitably identifying gifted students. *Gifted Child Quarterly* 65:3.

Lo. C. Own, Ph.D. et al. *Giftedness in the Making: A Transactional Perspective* in the *Gifted Child Quarterly*, 2019. 63:3 p. 172-184)

Twenge, Jean M., Ph.D. *iGen: Why Today's Super-Connected Kids are Growing Up Less Rebellious, More Tolerant, Less Happy—and Completely Unprepared for Adulthood.* Atria: 2017.

Walter, Jennifer. 2019. Audiobooks or reading? To our brains, it doesn't matter. *Discover Magazine*. Online at https://www.discovermagazine.com/mind/audiobooks-or-reading-to-our-brains-it-doesnt-matter

Chapter 5
In the Classroom: Let's Get Practical

The Four Word Mission Statement originally appeared in the NAGC blog at NAGC.org.

How to Kill a Passion Project originally appeared in the Fall 2020 issue of NAGC's Teaching for High Potential

The Four Word Mission Statement

How many hours have you and your colleagues spent agonizing over, sorting through, crafting, wordsmithing, cutting, pasting, and re-writing a mission statement? Maybe I can save you some trouble if you are a gifted resource teacher working on a mission statement for your classroom. I think you need only four words: *I love a challenge.*

For my gifted and talented classroom, these words pack all the necessary meaning inside—my teaching goals, my kids' ownership of the work they do, and even the social-emotional lessons inside any good Gifted and Talented Education (GATE) program.

I LOVE is both a proclamation and an expectation.

Does your classroom encourage a wiggly open-ended festival of differentiated choices? Our upper elementary students enjoy open-ended choices as well as dozens of menu choices in order to meet advanced learning plan goals. You want to learn more about cartooning techniques so you can expand your own series of superhero comics? Cool! You want to learn about microbes? Why not! Perhaps you'll LOVE our menus instead. Our middle schoolers LOVE the menu choices as ways to express their understanding. Can you navigate your way through the Spy Training Academy? How about designing propellers for WWII fighters? Can your prototype of a smoke jumper's parachute float accurately into a wildfire to help establish a fire line? You'll need to diagram the wildfire's progress from a bird's eye view and calculate the percentage of the area that has been damaged as well. This is serious simulation here! Students work diligently to meet the goal they've outlined in their Advanced Learning Plan (ALP). Once met, kids continue to work diligently on subsequent goals. We're never done…not really…we're just in different stages of improvement! We want passions to show, intensities to help gifted students shine: I LOVE can be played out every day.

Whole Kids—Not Just Test Scores

As a gifted resource teacher, I'm sure you often talk about pursuing one's passions and about how those passions don't have to fit inside a classroom. Many of my GATE students are very academic in the classic sense of the word, but many are not. Remember that we want our GATE classroom to be a place where kids feel safe to be who they are around like-minded peers. Look, it's OK to be a little nerdy here, a little intense, a little off-kilter. It's OK to be consumed by dragons or horses or baseball or math or lightsabers or even some sort of strange combination which puts all of these topics together—like hitting baseballs with a lightsaber while riding a horse and calculating your batting percentage. It's OK to have memorized the details of every interesting logo. It's OK to want to build and build and build and design and build some more. Whatever your passion or your disposition or your twice and thrice exceptionality, the same question remains: "What does the I LOVE part of learning feel like?" It feels exciting; it feels engrossing; it feels like you want more and more. It feels like choice. It feels safe and personal. It feels like home.

A CHALLENGE is both an academic requirement and a way of healthy living.

Maybe this GATE classroom feels a bit like fun and games, at times. Good! We call that kind of learning *flow*. You're supposed to have fun! You're supposed to love what you're doing, and we hope everyone continues to do so the rest of their lives. We're not just an advanced learning plan and a graduation gown. This giftedness is all-consuming and operates on thousands of frequencies…and it never stops.

HOWEVER…if everything is easy all the time, then won't we forever be stuck somewhere in 2nd grade? If we don't understand how to create and connect with challenges, then how will we ever accomplish anything great? How will we ever make ourselves proud? How will we ever fulfill a dream? So many times, GATE kids do not understand what a challenge feels like, or they can become experts at avoiding challenges or cautiously accepting manageable ones. Well … dang…challenges feel a little unpleasant and sometimes a lot unpleasant! Sometimes challenges feel like a sick stomach. Then, hopefully with effort and not too much heartache, challenges start to feel better and better, even exciting. In the end, it feels like we've earned the right to be proud. Those feelings are *growth*. Those feelings are healthy. Down in the GATE room, we talk often about these things, and we should never let those thoughts get too far away in any social-emotional lesson. Our mantra is "Ability is a blessing, but achievement is earned."

Four words for a mission statement…I rather like that. I think I will delete all those other mission statement drafts.

How to Kill a Passion Project

An earlier version of "How to Kill a Passion Project" was published in *Teaching for High Potential*, NAGC, May 2021

I am drawn to investigate a laughing huddle of students in my classroom of 4th graders. Joelle stands in the center holding her project about naked mole rats, and her laughter in particular is the sort that fills up a room and invites everyone else to join in. In her project, three naked mole rat models on toy wheels race down lanes inside a cardboard box. In each race, the winning naked mole rat reveals information about these odd little animals. Special *starred* information cards mean a student gets to take home a baby naked mole rat Joelle has made as prizes. As someone who cares about gifted education, you must be cringing as you read this. Laughter…in a classroom? Unacceptable. Quirky kids sharing humor with other quirky kids just like them? A student following a passion interest and creating a game? Where was the essay, the trifold, and the cited sources? We cannot tolerate this!

I am sure you are alarmed about the recent trend of teachers allowing students time to work on "passion projects," setting aside class time for "genius hour," and encouraging choice through personalized learning. Fortunately, with 34 years of classroom experience, I am a uniquely qualified guide for effective methods to kill passion projects and stifle personalized learning of all kinds. We can't—after all—have every student racing around, diving into who knows what subject area, messing up notebooks, messing up the classroom, draining all of our craft supplies, smiling and laughing, and modelling for other kids an irresponsible joy in learning. My trusty teacher's toolkit will help you make sure you can put a stop to this nonsense in 7 easy steps:

1. Make sure students are doing it your way.

Not wanting to let even a moment of opportunity slip away, Joelle had gathered a notebook full of research about naked mole rats. She had come to school bearing color illustrations and had neatly bound her findings inside a white binder. It caught me off guard. Had I been thinking, I would not have paged through the notebook with all too obvious delight. Naked mole rats! Ha, ha, how wonderful! Oops… Instead, I should have explained to Joelle that this research was all well and good for a 4th grader, but was it in the proper format? Had she cited her sources and paraphrased properly? Of course, I would have shown her that she would need to re-copy all her information onto notecards using the coding system that I had developed in 1986. Never mind that students will have plenty of chances to learn the nuts and bolts of citations and research many times over in the K-12 curriculum. Never mind that they will learn these rules and methods the first time or second time through without ever needing to re-visit the topics. Never mind that later my colleagues in high school will lead fabulous inquiry-based learning projects across the curriculum. Turn around and these 10 year-olds will be irresponsible middle schoolers. Better safe than sorry!

2. Only allow topics adults would choose.

We need to be clear about how completely inappropriate the topic of *naked mole rats* is. *Naked*? Seriously, this can't be OK in a school (hee, hee) can it? Only the most irresponsible teacher would allow such a thing! Never mind that the student is reading from several sources and learning about mammals—probably from sources not specifically designed for young readers…way too challenging! Middle school teachers and gifted resource specialists, especially, take heed. We would not want these kids' quirky senses of humor translated into dangerous levels of self-expression. The next thing you know, you'll have a gifted 8th grade boy studying Yetis, gathering historical narratives, weighing the plausibility of the stories, and then taking a tongue-in-cheek view as he dresses up in a rented Yeti costume and films alleged sightings around town which include a Yeti peacefully reclining at a bus top while waiting for the downtown express. These sorts of *Monty Pythonesque* stabs at humor will ruin entire programs! I'm glad we kept such travesties quiet, because he might have sacrificed the huge scholarship he won four years later.

3. Stick your nose into the project as often as possible.

Many of my fellow educators may have no choice. Maybe your schedule is handed to you containing a required *genius hour*. If this is the case, you should monitor every step of a student's process. Don't trust kids with anything. I suggest that you allow only two or three choices for finished products—one of them being an essay and another possibly a PowerPoint with many nifty transitions. Also make sure the required tri-fold backboard is neatly decorated. For goodness sakes, whatever you do, don't hand a student Susan Winebrenner's *Product Choices Chart.* If you allow products which are interactive, hands-on, creative, or include games or distracting displays of some sort, you are risking negative influences on the entire school. Everyone will want to do this—even little brothers and little sisters and future generations of students. Your failure will have a wide-ranging consequence. Never sharing products is the safest way to proceed.

4. Quit playing around.

I know this seems obvious. Learning should not be fun, and if we are spending a bunch of time playing around, we are sacrificing time we might have been preparing for standardized tests. In a recent *Scientific American* article (Schomburg, 2019) an experienced elementary science teacher describes tinkering as "a place free from failure because failure is not even a part of the equation." He observes that his students became self-motivated and engaged while tinkering because they had no fear of risking a bad grade. Our gifted learners sometimes carry a debilitating fear of failure—a key component in perfectionism. Therefore wouldn't it be a good idea to make sure that any passion project receives a weighty grade? Students should follow the most difficult social-emotional path, right? We have to quit coddling kids—even if it leads to miserable experiences with learning.

I sat down with two of my students to find out more. Nikolle (a 5th grader identified for giftedness in nonverbal ability) and Joelle (of the naked mole rats project) both agreed on the two most important features of a passion project. First, project choices allow them to study topics they love. Second, if their project doesn't go the way they want it to go, then they are free to change anything and everything about their study without worrying about someone else's requirements. Both students are frequent users of "studio time" in my classroom—up to three hours at the end of the week in which students are encouraged to pursue learning in their style and based on their curiosity. Both students—like most gifted students—are also their own harshest critic with the topics they love.

During studio time, the only person looking over their shoulders and monitoring what they are doing is another gifted kid—and that kid is usually encouraging what they see. Free from the fear of evaluation, students are free to love learning. As Jessica Lahey writes in her book, *The Gift of Failure* (2015), some children within the school system have "sacrificed (their) natural curiosity and love of learning at the altar of achievement, and it's our fault."

I am humble enough to admit my failure in offering studio time. During this time, Nikolle, a true dragon aficionado, has developed several dragon-themed projects. I often catch her doing research, both in books and online. This spring, she invented "dragon skins"—art pieces which turned regular printer paper into colorful and crispy "skins" with ink and water. Now the entire 5th grade and several 4th graders are making dragon skins just for the fun of it. I even caught a young and vulnerable 1st grader looking at the dragon skins with interest. Nikolle is reading what must be her 25th novel about dragons when she could have been reading district-adopted textbooks instead. Where will it end? Let' make sure kids are always working in isolation and completely within the curriculum. Laughter is as uncomfortable as exploration and sharing.

Together last school year during studio time, Nikolle and Joelle created supplementary stories, the beginnings of a novel, new characters, "cat" clans, dioramas, and adventures based on the *Warriors* series (including a quiz developed by Joelle to discover which Warrior clan one would be a part of—I would be RiverClan, I am proud to say). Several times, I saw other students gathered around the girls, asking questions, and offering positive comments. Several other kids got hooked on the *Warriors* series which, most unfortunately, had been donated to my classroom by 7th graders who had become hooked on the series 10 years before. See what I mean about ruining future generations of learners? We can't have that sort of legacy in the gifted and talented department!

5. Set limits.

I think of my own mistakes as a kid here. In the summer of my 5th grade year, our small-town librarian announced to me that we had no more books about baseball in the library. "You've read them all," she said, "even the adult books you shouldn't have read." Sadly, I had no responsible adult setting limits in my life and requiring me move on to other topics I didn't like so much. If I'd been influenced by a responsible adult, I would never have ruined by life majoring in English, would never have followed my father's footsteps into the classroom, and would never have ruined so many other kids' lives as well as my own.

6. Start with the standards and stick to them.

Simply stated, if a passion project does not clearly address a state or district standard (one you can itemize, number, and label), then it clearly has nothing to do with learning. It's time to move on. It would be horrible if teachers helped kids already deep in a project fit their learning to standards retroactively—mark the "met academic goal' on their advanced learning plans—and then keep right on learning. What if—and this makes me sad to even write—a project was matched to a standard AFTER the project was completed? Nope. I don't even want to go there…

You may remember that I taught middle school in a large, mixed urban/suburban district once upon a time. Poorly attended brown bag lunches and field trips had comprised the school's gifted program. With the support of an understanding administrator, we began to transform the gifted program to an enriching curricular program which met every day in the former Home Economics classroom. Gifted students came to me every day for reading class. It was agreed that I would use our 50 minutes together each day to teach much more than reading. "I know you will do whatever you need to do with our gifted kids," my principal told me over and over, "and you have my blessing."

We worked one to two years ahead of grade-level reading standards, often achieved mastery after one or two repetitions, and bought ourselves plenty of extra time. We used part of that "much more than reading" and "whatever you need to do" for independent projects which we showcased each spring. The showcase became the academic highlight of the year. What began as a few gifted kids sharing a few creative, interactive products eventually became a lively evening. Families and grandparents, friends, teachers, and pride—oh, so much pride in displaying one's abilities—filled the library. Former students returned from high school to view the projects. Let's also note that our standardized test scores became stronger very quickly. I truly believe this increased achievement was partly due to pride and the power of choice—a sense of "this is what we do, and this is who we are, and who we are involves showing our abilities."

In the end, I learned how to sincerely celebrate success, and I figured out more and more how to simply get out of the way.

References

Lahey, J. (2015, August 15). *When Success Leads to Failure*. Retrieved March 22, 2019, from https://www.theatlantic.com/education/archive/2015/08/when-success-leads-to-failure/400925/

Schomberg, A. (2019, February 20). *The Value of Tinkering*. Retrieved March 22, 2019, from https://blogs.scientificamerican.com/observations/the-value-of-tinkering/

Winebrenner, S. (2001). *Teaching Gifted Kids in the Regular Classroom: Strategies and Techniques Every Teacher Can Use to Meet the Academic Needs of the Gifted and Talented*. Minneapolis, MN: Free Spirit Publishing.

Appendix
Lessons and Units for Gifted Learners

More than a decade ago, one of my colleagues asked if I could share one of my creative units I no longer used so that she could add some variety to her language arts classroom. I was happy to...only I discovered that I couldn't. I had been writing my own lessons and units for many years, but when I opened my filing cabinet, I found that I hadn't actually *written* the units. They were on smudgy overhead projector slides, jotted down in calendars, or merely collections of notes and visuals and sample products. Shortly thereafter, I started not only writing my ideas but also publishing them. Since 2014, I have published over 225 lessons or units designed specifically for gifted learners, three gifted curriculum books, and have three more on the way. If the three units and additional menu choices published here don't fit your needs, then you can find a couple hundred more on my website at www.giftedlearners.org. Many of them are free, and all of them are ready to download and begin using right away.

The three units that appear below have been some of the most successful units I've taught, and I think they are appropriate (perhaps with some modifications) for students in grades 3 through 7th grade gifted and talented. They have been written specifically for gifted learners and offer activities and products that are creative, open-ended, and appeal to the wide abilities of our GenZ and our digital native learners.

I've chosen **Film Noir** as a full unit to share with you—chosen it with a bit of a sly smile. I know many of you gifted teachers out there are eclectic and quirky. Admit it! So why not have your kids learn about film noir? Yes...the pinnacle for eclectic and quirky cool! This multi-faceted, technology and media-enhanced unit will have your kids wanting to grow goatees, watch vintage Humphrey Bogart movies, drink espresso, wear berets, attend poetry slams, listen to NPR, and read Dostoevsky. Plus, just think of all the fun you'll have answering this question: "So...what are your GT kids doing?" Our highly visual GenZ kids should love this!

Two of the lessons which follow are social-emotional. **Tailwinds** is written specifically for gifted girls and presents a wonderful opportunity to invite your older gifted girls to mentor your younger girls through the lesson. Once upon a time, I invited former female students of mine—positive role models from the high school—to lead this lesson. As the "boy," I stepped out of the way and switched classrooms with one of my female colleagues (it's not hard to find a gifted girl who has become an elementary teacher) for the duration of the lesson.

I did not develop **Doodles** specifically for boys, but it is a wonderful way to engage boys in social-emotional understandings. I have been giving this unit away to participants in my professional development sessions about gifted boys for several years now (similarly, I often give Tailwinds away to educators who attend my gifted girls' sessions). Like all of my social-emotional units, I want to engage students with creativity, products, and curricular challenges that reach far beyond "let's sit down and talk." My boys rarely want to sit down and talk, but they love to create and play. P.S. —the girls have loved Doodles too.

How many times have your colleagues in the regular classroom asked, "What do I do with this gifted kid? He/she/they are way beyond what we're doing and is speeding through the curriculum." The answer is never easy, but the cubes are something to make your life a bit easier—something you can hand to them—as a starter. The Magical Gifted and Talented Cube Menu assignments are also effective in helping your gifted students generate ideas for independent passion projects. The cubes are not simply menus, though. They offer a wide variety of choices depending upon the ways in which they are used—all of which are explained in the unit.

Maddie and Tae's

Fly

A Social-Emotional Lesson for Gifted Girls

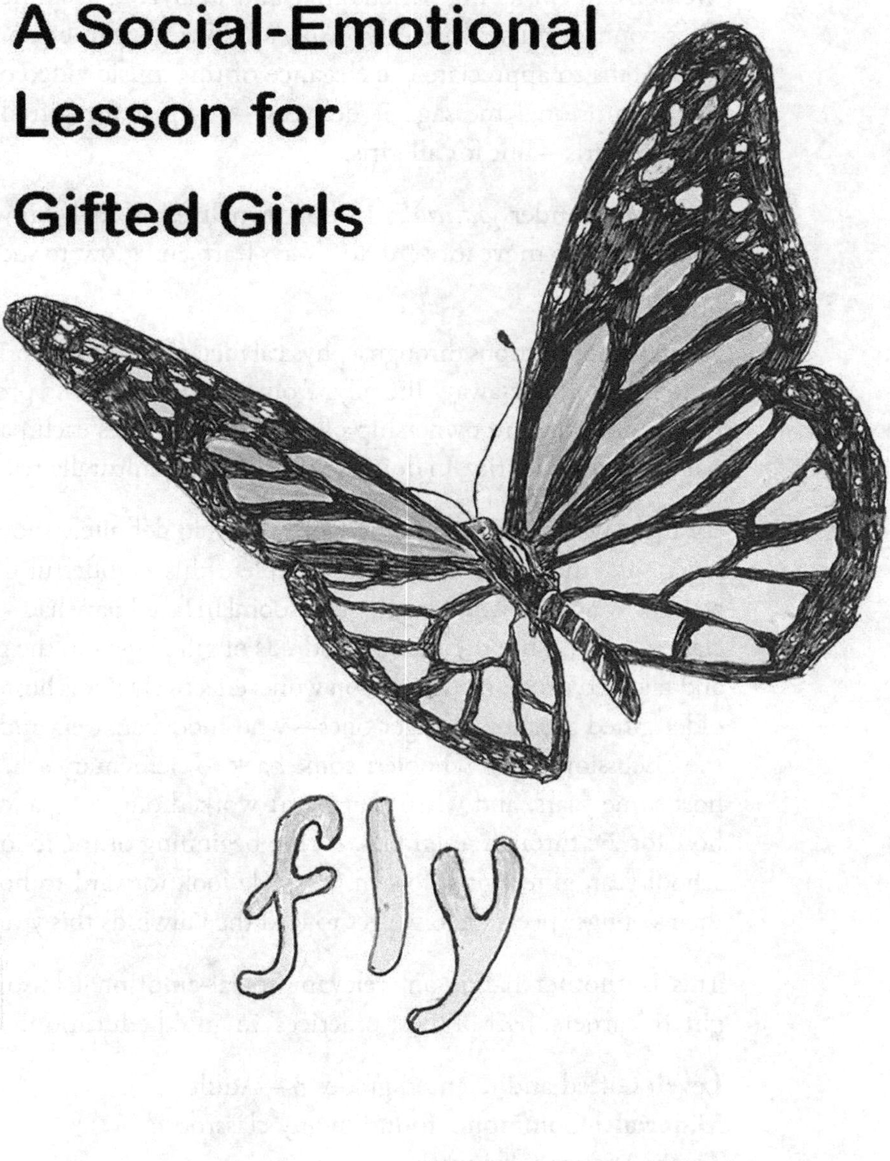

"Tailwinds" are people, abilities, talents, situations, environments, attitudes, and behaviors in our lives which empower us to succeed.

Psychological research shows us that healthy, positive, happy individuals understand the momentum these people and environments—these tailwinds—bring into one's life.

We've wrapped together several activities here—strong lessons, thoughtful messages, and meaningful context for our gifted girls.

We start by watching, discussing, and analyzing Maddie and Tae's country music video, *Fly*. All y'all don't have to be country music fans to appreciate the elegance of this music video or the social-emotional message it delivers—not just for gifted and talented girls—but for all girls.

Next, we ponder *gratitudes* in our own lives. Which tailwinds empower us to move forward, to always learn and grow, to succeed, to fly?

We make connections through a physical metaphor—a cool origami butterfly as a take-away (literally) from the lesson. In the process, personalization and ownership of the lesson touches each participant's unique identity. In doing so, the lesson is culturally relevant.

If I had a classroom full of gifted girls, I would definitely show this video, ask these questions, and complete this wonderful design activity. Wait. . .I have had such a classroom! In fact, I have had several classrooms and hundreds and hundreds of gifted girls in the gifted and talented program. This lesson works effectively if it is hosted by older gifted girls for younger ones—who model answers and lead the discussion. High schoolers come back to elementary school to host some years, and when that hasn't worked out, 5th grade girls host for 2nd through 4th grades. At the beginning of the following school year, gifted girls now in 5th grade look forward to hosting their younger peers. "Do we get to lead the tailwinds this year?"

This is another hands-on, relevant social-emotional lesson for gifted learners, part of 'best practices' in gifted education.

Level: Gifted and talented grades 3—Adult
Materials: Commonly found in any classroom
Time: About 90 minutes

Fly—Opening Video Analysis Activity

I suggest watching the video once through and gathering general impressions first. Then view the video a second time for the critical thinking questions.

The synergy of group discussion is very strong in this activity; however, you might consider assigning various questions to small groups before coming together as a class to discuss all the questions.

Isn't it almost magical—at times—the insights you get from your students? Allow discussion to go outside the lines of the questions below if it takes that direction. I love the leaps and connections of the gifted brain. You will likely find, like I did, that students jump ahead of you and start commenting on questions you haven't even asked yet.

Your girls will most likely surprise you with insights and observations. There are no "correct" answers to the critical thinking questions; however, students should support their answers with details from the video and/or the lyrics.

Video Link: https://www.youtube.com/watch?v=KfDr_7LN-Ew

If the link changes down the road, search for the music video, Maddie and Tae, *Fly*.

Critical Thinking Questions

- What meanings do you associate with the word "fly?" What other words are associated with this word?
- Explain the meaning of these lyrics: "You can learn to fly on the way down."
- One of the interesting visual choices the director makes is featuring different chairs suspended on a wall. What do the chairs represent? Is it important that each chair is different?
- Maddie and Tae are sitting in suspended chairs. We don't know this at first, but it is revealed later in the video. What effect does this director's decision have on the viewer?
- One might argue that sitting in these suspended chairs represents life and its choices. How so? Is this a positive or a realistic view of life?
- List as many video references as you can find for *climbing* or *being suspended*. Why are they included in the video?
- Can you think of another video clip of climbing that might also be used if you were the writer/director of this video?
- A butterfly is often featured in the video? Why? Is this a good choice? Would some sort of bird be a better choice?
- Explain these lyrics: "You won't forget the heavy steps it took to let it go."
- Brain researchers have commented that gifted learners in particular can remember negative words and interactions years later. Do you find this to be true? Does this relate to "let it go?"
- Why are girls and women of various ages featured?
- How are the girls and women depicted? What inferences can you make about them? Are these positive depictions? Are they accurate?
- At one point, a mother stops and thinks as she looks at her daughter. Why does the director choose to include this moment? What do you think the mother is thinking?
- Is your mother a gifted learner? Have you talked to her about her experiences at your age?

- ❍ What is the overall mood or tone of this video? Cite examples to support your answer.
- ❍ What do you think about the color and costume choices made for the video? Do they match the theme?
- ❍ Explain these lyrics: "Just keep on climbing though the wind might break."
- ❍ How are the last seconds of the video constructed to deliver a positive message? Contrast these seconds to the opening scenes of the video.
- ❍ If all the scenes and images in the video were positive, would it enhance or detract from the message or theme of the video?
- ❍ According to the lyrics and the video, how should we approach life? Or…is it worth risking falling from a chair?
- ❍ Is the theme of the video and song a universal message, or do you think it is specifically for girls and women?

Get your toolkit for engaging students from Generation Z here—FREE. It's designed for critical thinking and analysis of all things visual:

https://www.teacherspayteachers.com/Product/Engaging-iGen-GENERATION-Z-with-Visuals-Videos-Toolkit-and-Lessons-FREE-GATE-4215936

Creating Powerful Physical Metaphors

Having discussed the video, let's internalize our understanding by creating a physical, tangible metaphor—an origami butterfly.

"Tailwinds" are people, abilities, talents, situations, environments, attitudes, and behaviors in our lives which empower us to succeed.

Psychological research shows us that healthy, positive, happy individuals understand the momentum these people and environments—these tailwinds—bring into one's life. For an interesting discussion about Tailwinds, listen to the Freakonomics podcast, *Why is My Life so Hard*, linked below.

Use the graphic organizer further below and the sample response to help students brainstorm tailwinds which propel them forward in life.

After students have completed the planner, they will further reinforce the metaphor by folding a paper butterfly labelled with their own tailwinds to represent their personal power to succeed—to fly.

http://freakonomics.com/podcast/why-is-my-life-so-hard/

Name________________________

Tailwinds

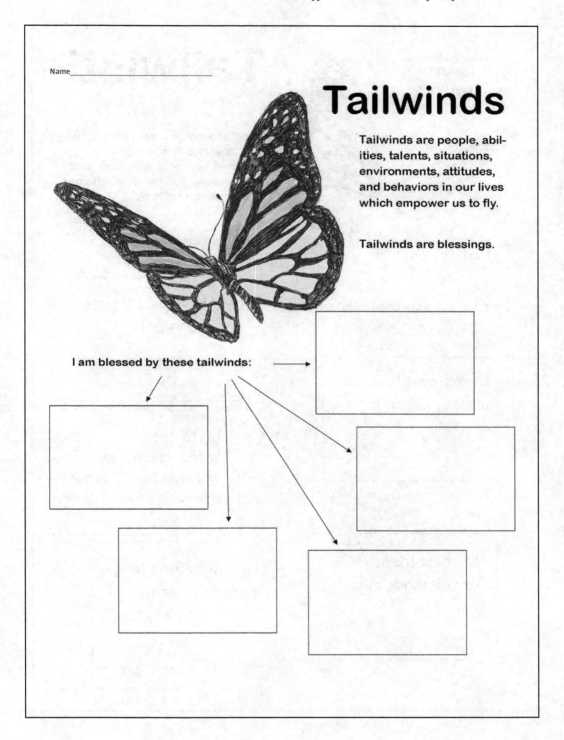

Tailwinds are people, abilities, talents, situations, environments, attitudes, and behaviors in our lives which empower us to fly.

Tailwinds are blessings.

I am blessed by these tailwinds:

SAMPLE ANSWERS

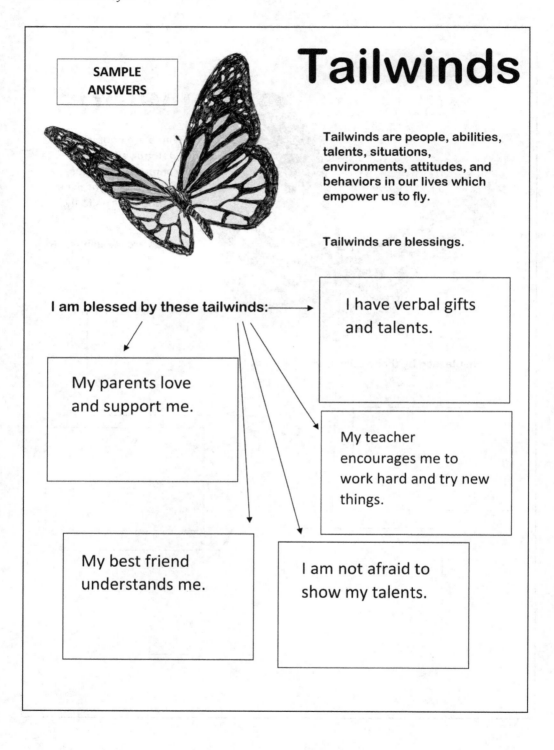

Tailwinds

Tailwinds are people, abilities, talents, situations, environments, attitudes, and behaviors in our lives which empower us to fly.

Tailwinds are blessings.

I am blessed by these tailwinds:

I have verbal gifts and talents.

My parents love and support me.

My teacher encourages me to work hard and try new things.

My best friend understands me.

I am not afraid to show my talents.

Why are we making little paper butterflies? Isn't this just a "cutesy" teacher post for Pinterest?

Because discussion about visual and physical observations links the hemispheres of the brain—strengthening learning through a "crisscross" of verbal and visual thinking...

Because our 21st Century learners tend to orient themselves visually and are skilled with spatial relationships...

Because our high ability nonverbal learners may understand better through experiencing the world around them and drawing conclusions about what they observe...

Because as visually-spatially oriented learners, our high ability nonverbal learners and 21s Century kids benefit from expressing understanding through graphic organizers which serve as an important link between fostering a visual-language connection...

Because hands-on activities are high interest and good for both kinesthetic and visual learning styles...

Because planning and creating an origami butterfly—in this context—is creating a meaningful physical metaphor.

With the *gratitudes* planned and in place, prepare to personalize the responses by folding a paper butterfly.

First, make a colorful pattern from a square of paper. Included below is a template which may be used…or freestyle the design. Tip: use lighter colors so the *tailwind* labels stand out.

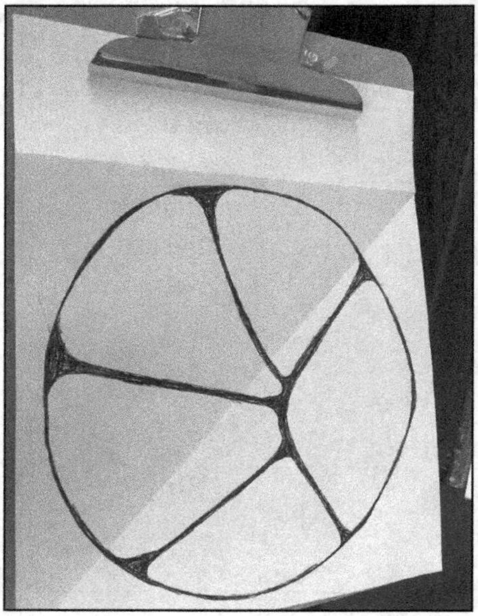

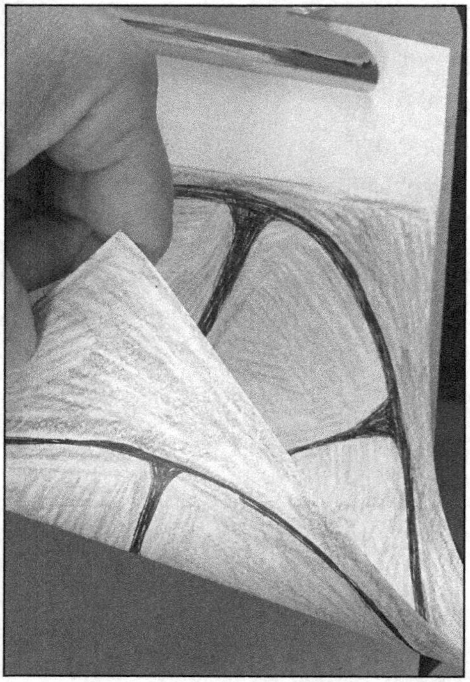

Now fold the butterflies to create the physical metaphor. I have found this video to be easy to follow. There are others if you do a little exploring.

https://www.youtube.com/watch?v=cZdO2e8K29o

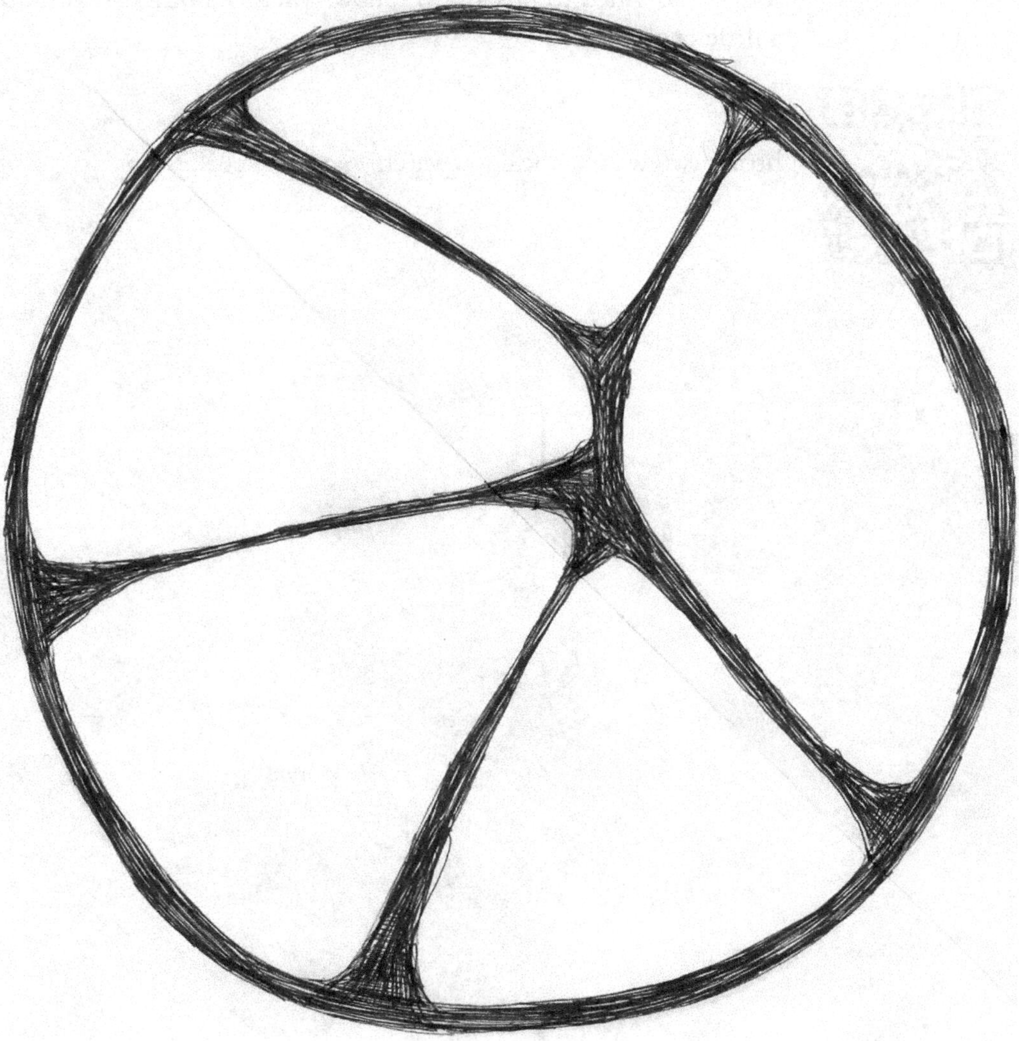

Once the butterfly is created, add the gratitudes to the wings to create the take-away from the lesson.

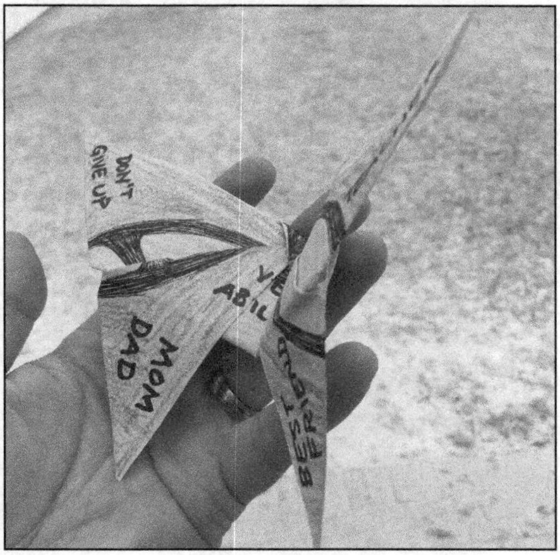

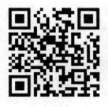

For a cool, more difficult paper folding challenge, try this one:

https://www.youtube.com/watch?v=TmvWB3SXpnE

Ways to Support Gifted Girls

adapted from *When Gifted Kids Don't have all the Answers*
by Jim Delisle and Judy Galbraith

- Identify early—between ages 3 ½ to 7
- Provide stimulating and challenging programs
- Encourage higher-level math and science
- Use multiple measures of achievement
- Encourage pride in taking credit for success and achievements
- Provide positive role models in literature and texts
- Foster connections with gifted peers
- Provide positive role models in the professional world
- Avoid sex-role stereotyping
- Encourage independence
- Encourage risk-taking
- Maintain the same expectations for boys and girls

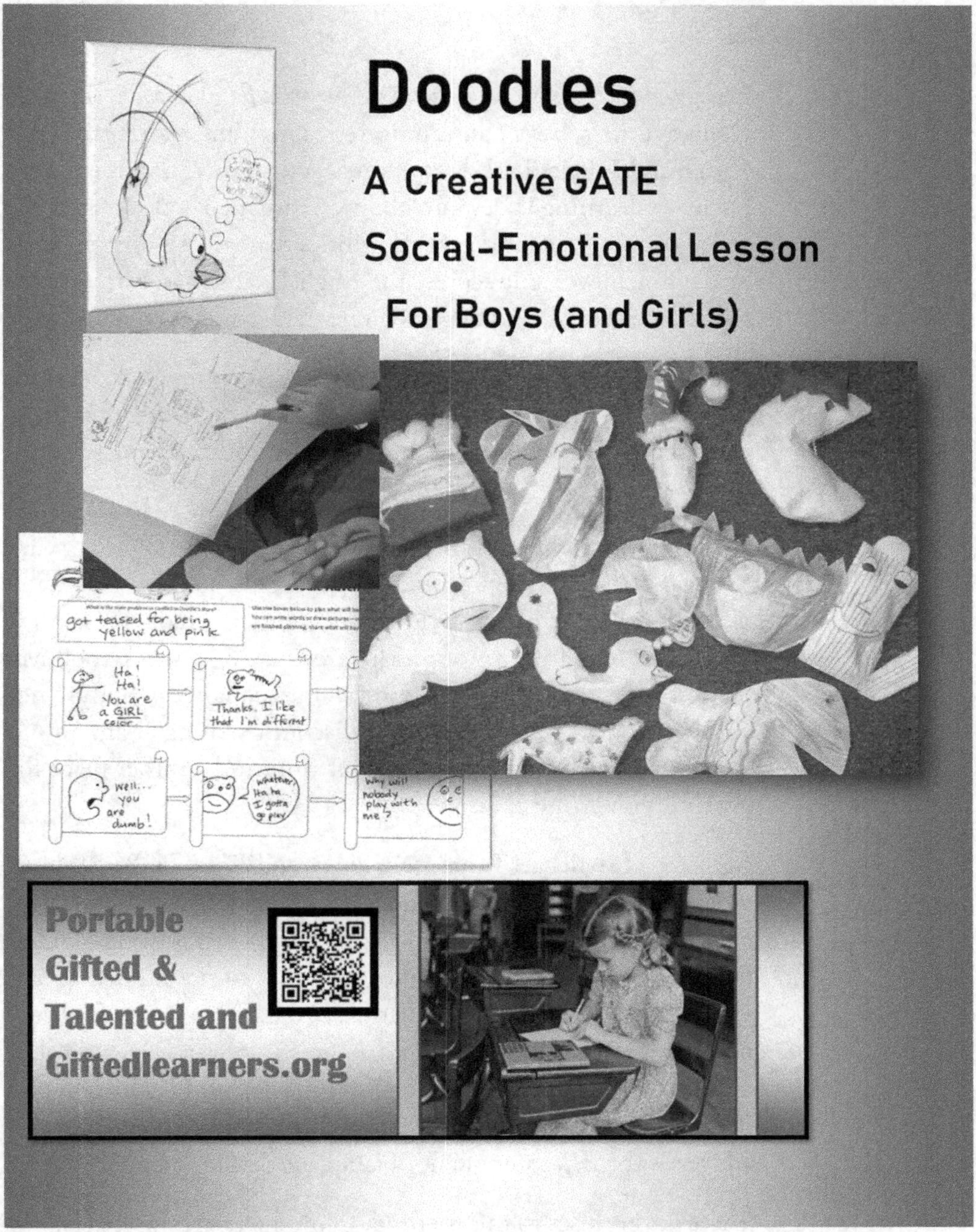
Doodles
A Creative GATE
Social-Emotional Lesson
For Boys (and Girls)
got teased for being yellow and pink
Ha! Ha! You are a GIRL color.
Thanks. I like that I'm different
Well... you are dumb!
whatever, Ha ha... I gotta go play
Why will nobody play with me?
Portable Gifted & Talented and Giftedlearners.org

Doodles Creative Social-Emotional Lesson

Designed to speak in *boy language (but good for girls, too!)*: this unit is built to help boys communicate feelings and participate in a Gifted and Talented social-emotional activity. The unit is effective for many learning styles and abilities: visual-spatial for students strong in nonverbal and general abilities that may be unsupported by high achievement scores, for English language learners, for twice-exceptional, and engaging creativity for everyone.

You've heard about child psychologists using puppets to get kids to open up? Think of this lesson in the same way—except infused with depth and complexity and creativity and academics.

We use storytelling instead of writing for bringing to life Doodle's adventures in my GATE pull-out group. I am specifically trying to engage boys, and I am working with the assumption that many of our boys are reluctant writers in 2nd and 3rd grade. (Yes, yes, I have some boys in my groups who are amazing writers, too!) My focus in gifted and talented, however, is to enhance A-bility—not emphasize IN-ability. We do not discount writing, I am an old English teacher. But there is another time and another place for developing writing skills.

According to Michael Thompson, Ph.D. and Teresa H. Barker in *It's a Boy* (p. 210), 4/5^{ths} of elementary school instruction is language-based. Many boys say they dislike reading and writing—gifted boys included. Boys need to move around, to use humor, to use improvisation and act out situations: "the central issue for boys, no matter what subject is being taught, are movement, control of choice, variety, (and) interaction with the group" (Thompson and Barker, p. 217). *Doodles* provides each of these elements yet also addresses the key component of language development.

There are bonuses to this method. Our reluctant boy writers, our ELL students, our visual-spatial and image-oriented learners, and our twice-exceptional students all will be motivated as they make visual-language connections through planning character development and narrative graphic organizers. They will enjoy telling and performing their stories—acting them out if they choose—and cartooning their plans.

Not only will *Doodles* open the possibility of social-emotional lessons and provide academic depth in characterization and narratives, but *Doodles* is hugely reliant on creativity.

Search the keyword *creativity* and you'll find a flood of hits—many of them explaining how creativity can be harnessed to increase production, innovation, and yield bigger profits. It's not hard to imagine why *creativity and innovation* is a key component to 21st Century learning.

In the *creativity* portion of the *Doodles*, students use imagination and multiple perspectives to transform doodles into pictures. This process is not only fun but also stretches a student's creative skills through the creative components of flexibility and originality.

21st Century Learners need purposeful creativity in order to be productive citizens, and the narrative writing (optional), storytelling, and improvisation activities which follow provide a productive purpose for our doodle creativity—matched and aligned with content standards. Students provide elaboration to one of their doodle creatures, give it a personality, and take their *Doodle* on a narrative adventure.

Finally, students complete the unit with more fun and more hands-on challenge as they create a 3D art piece in the *stuffed doodle* activity. Through this activity, *Doodle* comes to life!

Note: This lesson does not include a grading rubric. Individual grade level, school, district, and state narrative writing grading rubrics are applicable to components of this storytelling activity.

Common Core Standards—sample from 4th grade; other grades fit accordingly

CCSS.ELA-Literacy.W.4.3
Write narratives to develop real or imagined experiences or events using effective technique, descriptive details, and clear event sequences.

CCSS.ELA-Literacy.
W.4.3a Orient the reader by establishing a situation and introducing a narrator and/or characters; organize an event sequence that unfolds naturally.

CCSS.ELA-Literacy.W.4.3b
Use dialogue and description to develop experiences and events or show the responses of characters to situations.

CCSS.ELA-Literacy.W.4.3c
Use a variety of transitional words and phrases to manage the sequence of events.

CCSS.ELA-Literacy.W.4.3d
Use concrete words and phrases and sensory details to convey experiences and events precisely.

CCSS.ELA-Literacy.W.4.3e
Provide a conclusion that follows from the narrated experiences or events.

Other Featured Competencies from 21st Century Learning include art and creativity.

Learn at http://www.battelleforkids.org/how-we-help/portrait-of-a-graduate

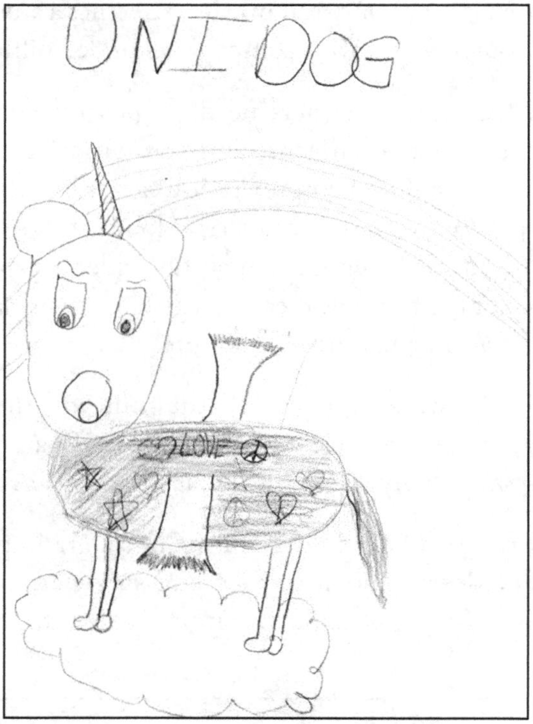

Activity One: Doodle Game

First, we must create a Doodle, and we'll begin our creation process through the "doodle game."

Demonstrate the doodle game by completing a doodle for the entire class from a *starter* doodle. "Starter" doodles must not take up too much space on a 1/4th rectangular section of paper (see box 1), must not have any crossed lines (see box 2), and must not be overly complicated (see box 3). Boxes one and four, shows a good "starter" doodle.

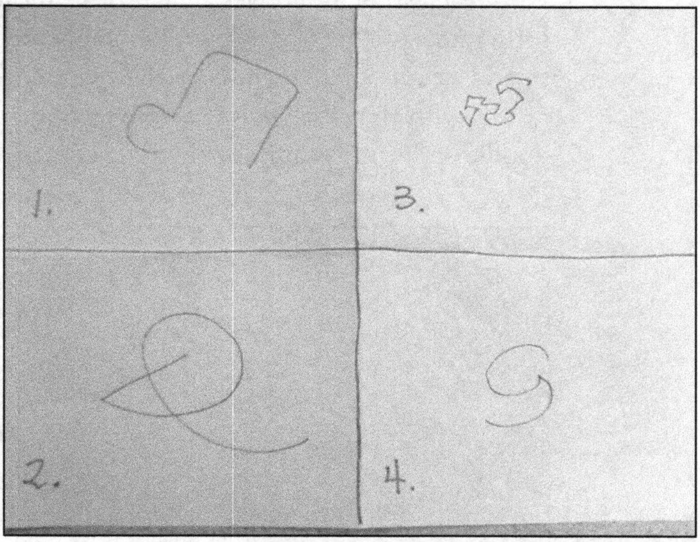

The next photo below shows a completed doodle from box 4. Encourage students to turn the "starter" doodle around in different directions and use their imagination and alternative perspectives for possible ways to complete the doodle. Encourage them to add words, details, and background to the picture. Encourage students to talk about their doodle and to tell a story with it if they can.

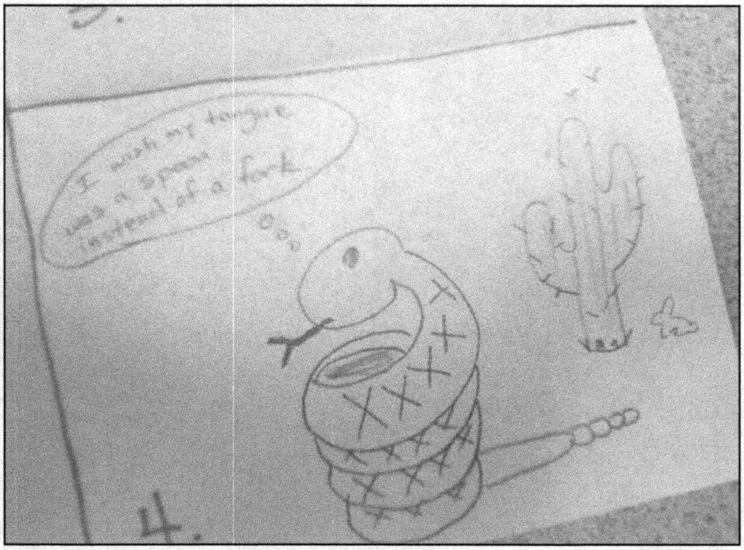

Next, each student receives an identical "starter" doodle to transform into a picture (see below). Remember to encourage students to add details or add words to the picture. Students share their results with the class. Below is one second grade class's "starter" doodle and some examples of students' work.

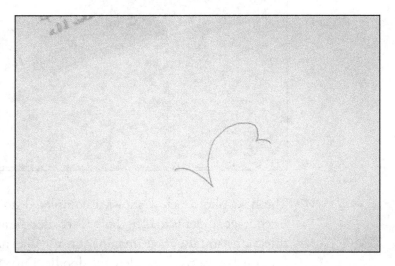

Can you find the ways the "starter" doodle was transformed into different pictures below and on the next page?

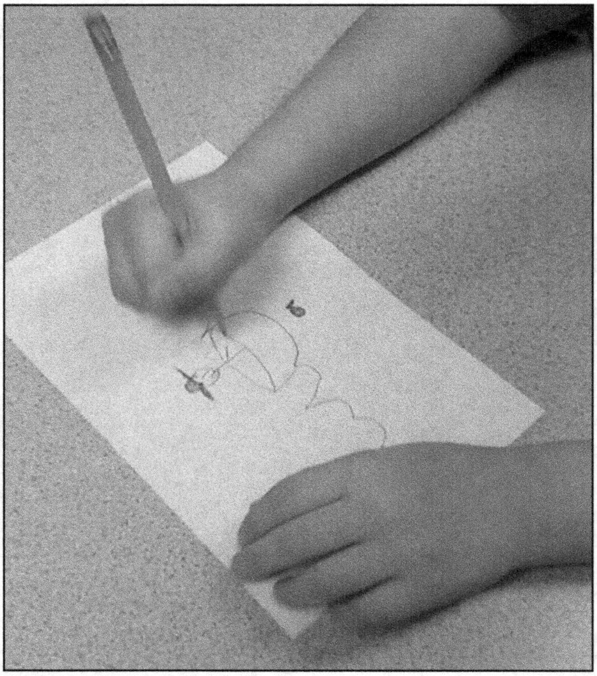

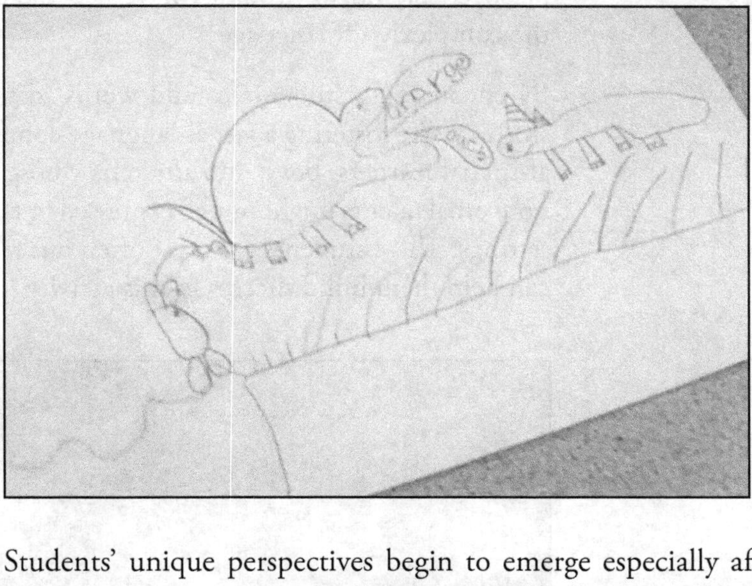

Students' unique perspectives begin to emerge especially after some encouragement. In the first drawing after the starter doodle, for example, this student eventually added wooden planks and nails to the boat along with other details. Great *elaboration*! Students with strong nonverbal ability often prove to be visually perceptive and can translate their unique talent for visual details into drawings.

The Visual-Language Connection

Encourage students to add words (last sample picture) as well as tell the class about their drawings. The main visual and language areas of the brain are on opposite hemispheres. Any time we can ask students to connect these hemispheres allows for better understanding and greater growth.

In addition, asking students (especially younger students) to talk about their work often lends insight into what we wouldn't necessarily understand at first glance. The student who presented the last sample picture told about a fight between a hippo and a rhino and piranhas jumping up out of the water to bite the *behind* of the hippo. The story was told with great enthusiasm and with vocal variety. Without the telling of the story, we would have missed out on some fun times and the student's unique perspective, and we wouldn't have had the opportunity to add the complexity of language.

By encouraging students to add words to their doodles or tell stories, we're fostering a visual-language connection for our visual-spatial learners, boys, and students whose general intellect or nonverbal talents might not be expressed in traditional classroom settings. These students are most often our reluctant writers. We can help them build success in this activity from the outset.

Finally, having practiced a bit and knowing the rules for starter doodles, students are ready to play the *doodle game*.

In order to play the doodle game, students fold a standard sheet of un-lined paper into four sections and "partner up" to play. Each partner draws a doodle "starter" for the other (making sure to follow the rules) in one of the four rectangles created by the folds. Partners then complete the doodles and share results with each other.

We use large 12" x 18" paper for even more room.

*Suggest that students make at least one "creature" out of the doodles. This is important for the storytelling activity.

Social-Emotional Follow-up Questions for Understanding—just a preview of important social-emotional work to come:

- ❍ Why do people imagine so many different things with the doodles?
- ❍ Why do people sometimes imagine almost identical things?
- ❍ Is one person's idea of a *doodle* better than another's?
- ❍ Why is it important that people have things in common?
- ❍ Why is it important that people are different and unique?
- ❍ What would you tell someone who told another person they didn't "like" that other person's imagination?
- ❍ What would you tell a student who insists they "can't think of anything" to make from the doodle "starter?"
- ❍ What would you tell another student who has quit the activity because they said none of their ideas are any good?

> The boy focus: Boys love to be problem-solvers and prefer to lend advice to others over talking about their own feelings. These last three questions open a social-emotional discussion about acceptance of others, diversity, and perseverance as well as perfectionism.

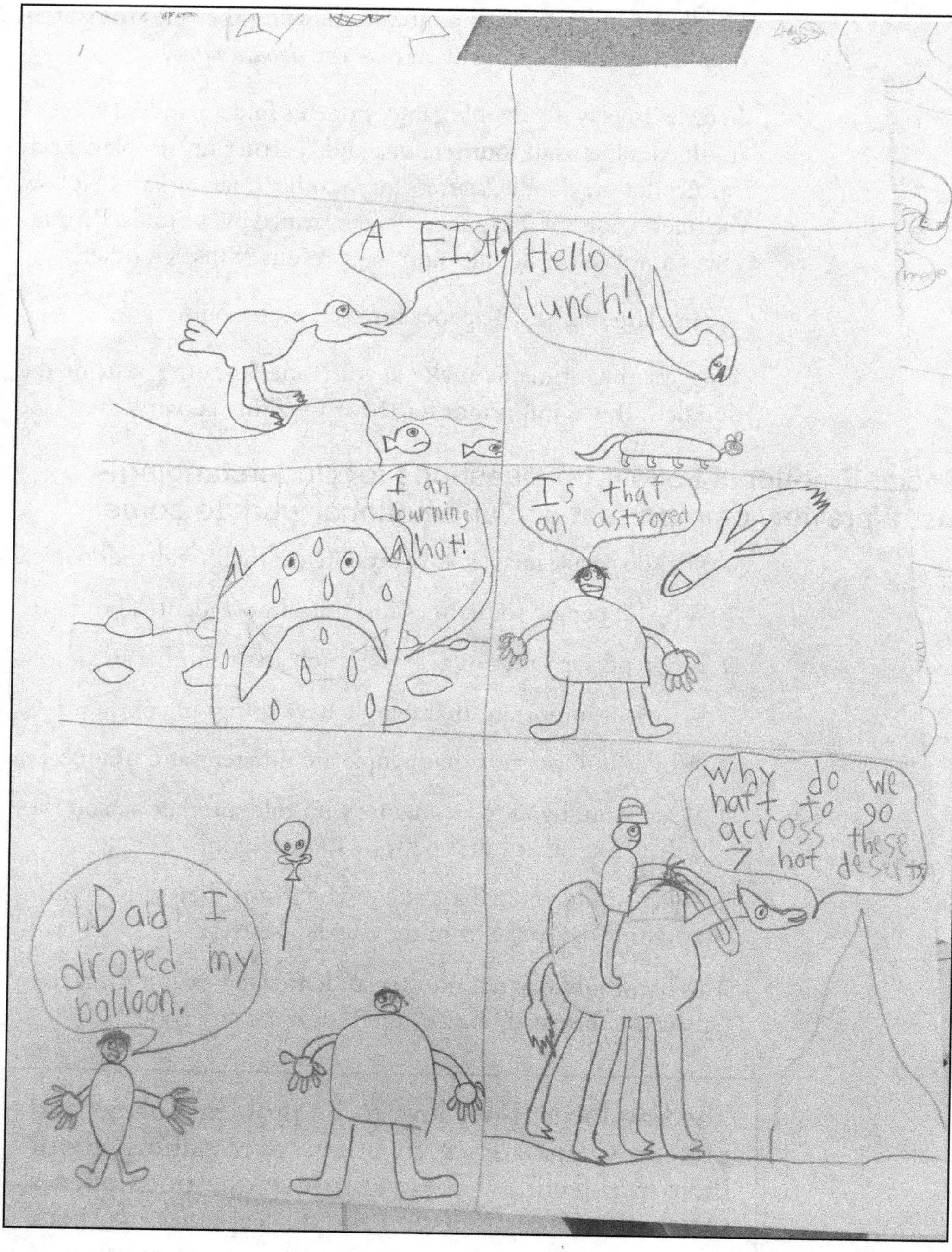
A FISH.
Hello lunch!
I an burning hat!
Is that an astroyed
LDaid I droped my balloon.
why do we haft to go across these 7 hot desets

The Magic of the Examples from the Teacher

Use examples which are social-emotional topics, and watch what happens!

While demonstrating the planning stages of the lesson, I discovered a *magical* method for engaging boys in a social-emotional lesson. I thought I was simply using humor to engage 2nd grade boys (and girls) while mixing in some discussion items, but it grew into much more.

You can see my two examples below. I used humor and then planned a story in which *Doodle* is teased on the playground. *Doodle* deals with the teasing with a lighthearted attitude and humor, and the bully doesn't know what to do.

Magic.

The students mimicked my example. They created *Doodles* and conflicts in similar ways. They loved it. They giggled through plans, and they giggled through artwork. They giggled through stories, and they giggled their way through social-emotional lessons. More examples are provided further below.

Wow! I had stumbled upon several effective ways of engaging boys in the important work of social-emotional lessons:

- Meeting gifted boys on their own *boy* terms because in so many important ways they are just like all other boys.
- Understanding that gifted boys may need help finding language to discuss feelings.
- Understanding that boys may not be willing to discuss feelings directly.
- Crafting safe avenues of discourse.
- Using humor and creativity and storytelling.
- Allowing boys to perform improvisations, move around, and role play and pretend they are not themselves.
- We encourage boys to talk about what *other* boys—fictional boys or Doodles—might do. We encourage them to counsel fictional boys through difficult situations on the playground, at home, and inside their own thoughts and feelings.

Activity Two: Planning and Telling/Performing the Doodle Adventure PLUS Social-Emotional Mini-Lessons

It's time to create narratives and examine social-emotional issues—adding the key components of elaboration and productive thinking to the creative process.

In this activity, students will plan an adventure for one of the doodles they've created and then tell the story to another student and/or the class.

Surely everyone has created some sort of creature (animal, human, or imagined) with one of their five doodle creations so far… Students will choose their favorite doodle as the main character in their narrative. One or two students may not have created a *creature*. If this is the case, can they make one of the doodles they have created *part* of a creature? This seems to work for my kids.

I actually had one student use a doodle that was a watering can. He gave the can a personality and voice, and it was delightful! (And a note from the introduction: this was the same student who once told me I was his second favorite teacher!)

Before we begin telling stories, let's begin developing our Doodle's character by completing the graphic organizer below. As students complete this first graphic organizer called *Doodle Comes to Life!,* they begin to generate ideas about which of Doodle's adventures they'll tell and the events that might take place. Watch the smiles begin…

Name______________________

Doodle Comes to Life!

What if your Doodle were a real-life creature who could speak to you, go to school, and do all of the normal day-to-day things in life? What would Doodle's personality be like? Would Doodle have and special skills? What challenges might Doodle face? Complete the graphic organizer below to help Doodle come to life.

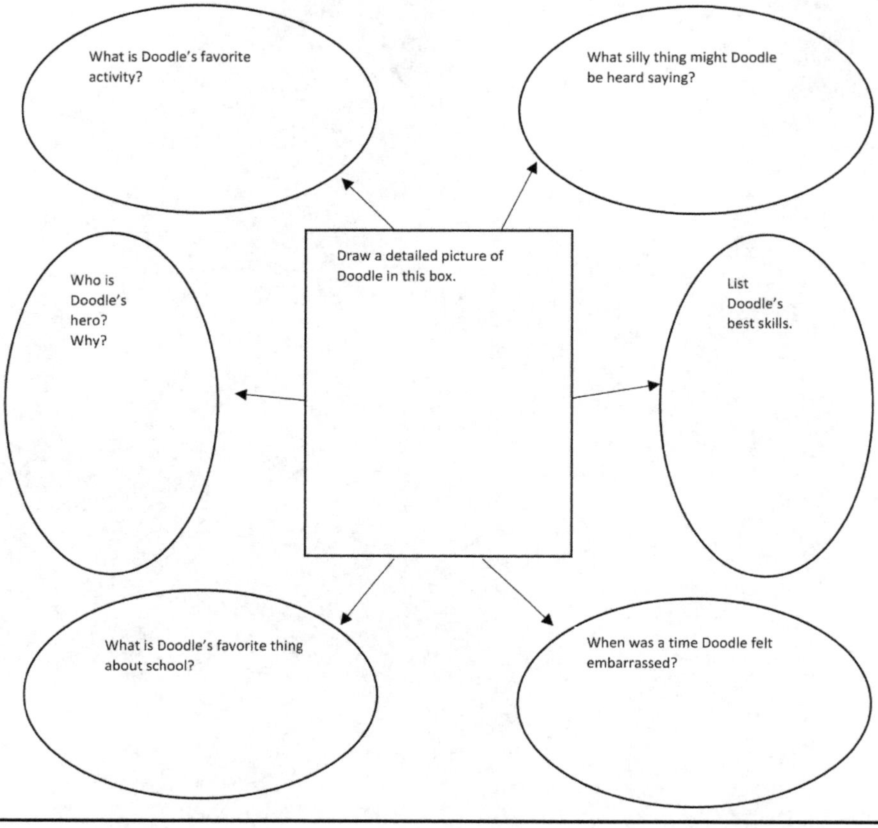

In the sample below, I named other students, Benson and Jalen, as someone *Doodle* admired because of his work ethic (not because of an ability). Each person in the class proceeded to name someone else in the class in their plans they admired, too—effectively affirming that classmate and virtually all the other students in the class in the process. What a place to call home—a place where someone may be oneself in the company of others who understand them—affirming once again the power of building relationships.

Why not make a classmate a hero? Why not fill the Doodle plans with individuality and unique qualities?

We also use humor—self-deprecating humor in some instances as a model to perfectionists in the making. We all love to laugh. School and life and hanging out together in the gifted and talented classroom is better with humor.

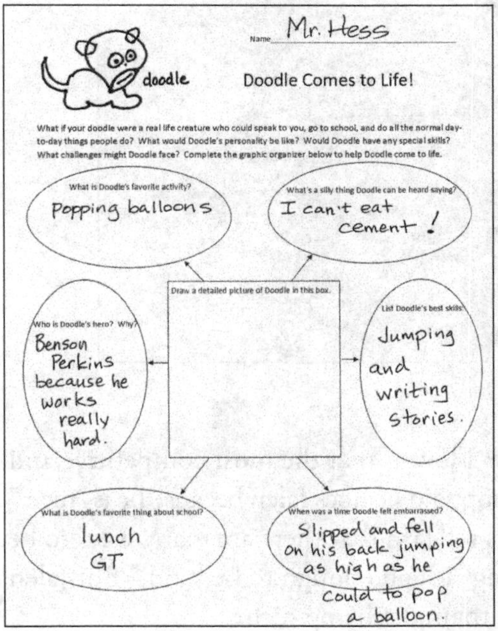

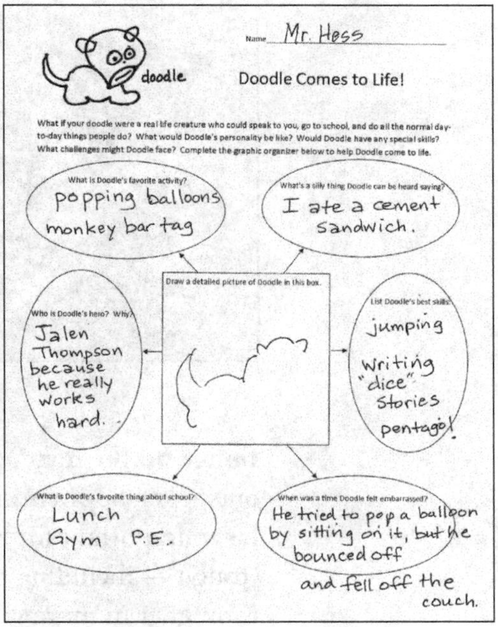

Below, you can see below samples of how students mimicked the model:

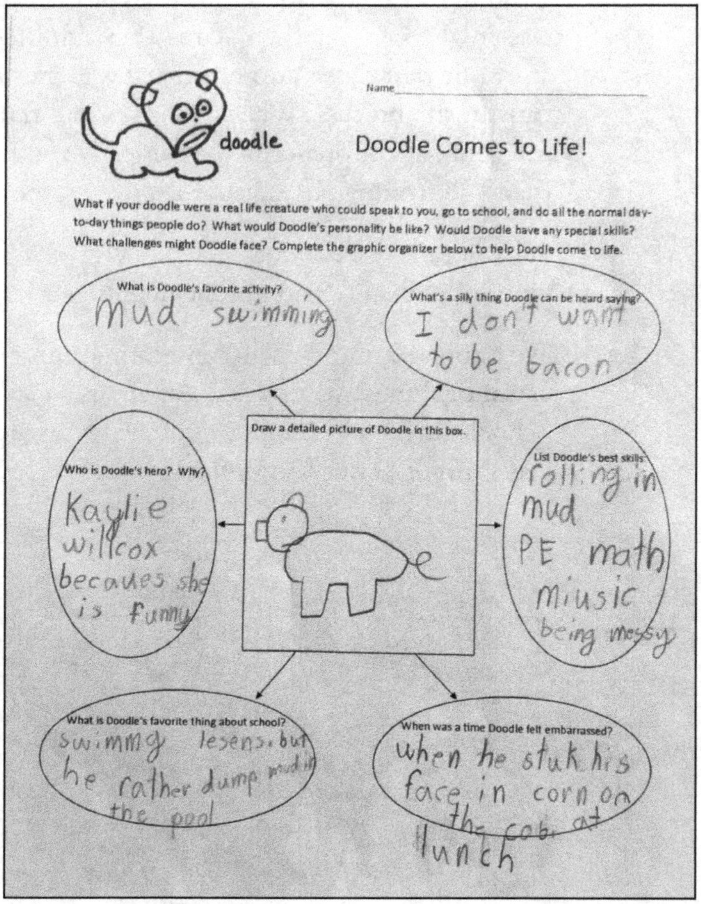

Image on the next page: I love it that the most competitive and outspoken boy in my group said he likes Jalen because he is "nice." It's so important for boys to learn that there are many ways to be "tough"—including being "tough enough to be kind." But Jalen is tougher in more ways than just being nice…

Remember the boy with Leukemia from the "This is How Boys are Tough" section? That's Jalen, and I am happy to report he is now cancer free…and he won a youth impact award for community service from the Colorado Association for Gifted and Talented along the way.

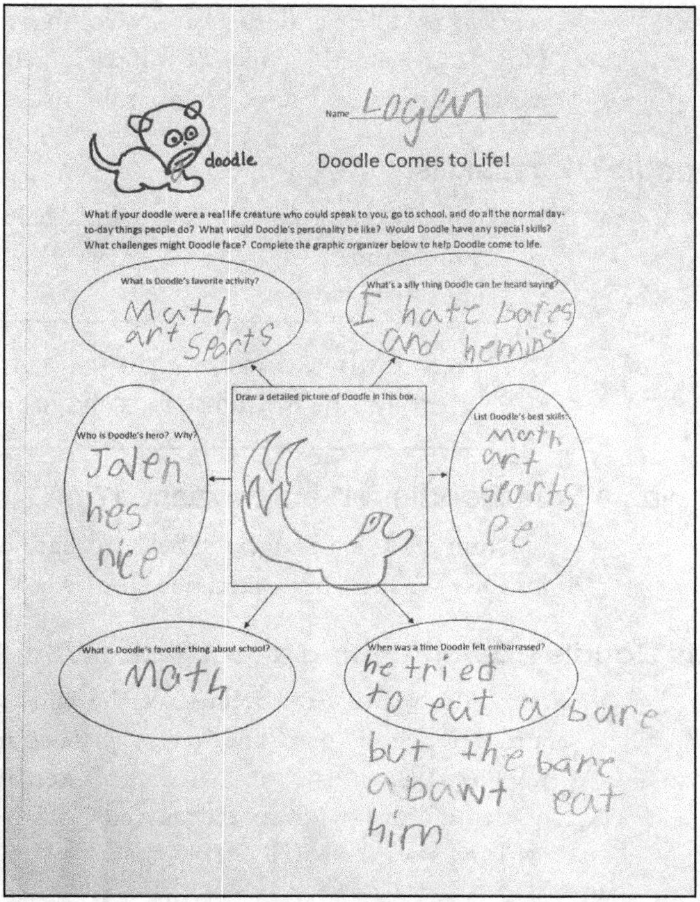

Let's make sure to load social-emotional items into the samples we provide. Remember, though, we want to have fun. Don't overdo the GATE social-emotional messaging. I recommend just 2 or 3 targeted concepts on your planner sample.

A few suggestions for each planning bubble:

Favorite Activity:

Choose something unique or really *nerdy* (I use that word lovingly). It's OK to be different! Choose something that crosses gender lines.

What is something Doodle can be heard saying?

Choose any social-emotional topic and match it with a quote. For example, if your topic is friendship, have Doodle say something like "Nobody likes me" (negative and at the heart of perfectionism) or "Hey, do you want to play?" (positive). If your topic is *saving the world* and the resulting feelings of helplessness, have Doodle say something like, "I will try to help the people around me any way I can. I hope others will join me."

List Doodle's best skills:

You might try some soft skills here like "being kind" or "being a good big brother."

> Remember, don't overdo it on the messaging. Remember to have fun.

When was a time Doodle felt embarrassed?

Use humor. The message will be clear that no one is perfect, and it's OK. We mess up sometimes, don't we?

What is Doodle's favorite thing about school?

Anything works here because of the wide variety of students' interests. I chose "gym" and "recess" just because I thought a lot of my boys would relate to it (true…a bit stereotypical, but I model academics for boys every day as well). Maybe I should have put "writing stories" as well.

Who is Doodle's hero? Why?

We've already discussed how this response can be used to affirm others in class. I like that model the best. We can, however, choose a person whose personal qualities are a good social-emotional lesson in themselves. How about something like this? "Doodle's Sister. She has a learning disability, and school is hard for her, but she always has a smile." Or this: "Jonas Salk. He invented the polio vaccine but refused to patent it because he wanted it to be free to everyone."

Planning the Story—Social-Emotional Prompts

Now it's time to plan Doodle's adventure. Ask the students to review the graphic organizer they've just completed. Ask questions like, "What sorts of challenge a creature like your Doodle might find in life?" "What would Doodle be good at?" "Would Doodle be a good friend or a good student? How could Doodle use its special talents to get out of trouble…or to get into trouble?!"

Let's help students focus an idea for their narrative into a social-emotional lesson. We use the seven prompts below as story starters which can help zero in on a social-emotional understanding. What if, however, some students want to write an adventure not covered by the topics? That's just fine! We don't want to use social-emotional lessons like a hammer or handcuffs. In the end, this lesson does not absolutely have to be a social-emotional one; however, through teacher modelling, the story is likely to be a response to key social-emotional issues on some level. The worst that can happen is that students tap their creativity and narrative skills to create a story. We can't lose.

1. Doodle gets in trouble at school because of a misunderstanding.
2. Doodle solves a conflict at recess.
3. Doodle feels bad about things in the world and tries to help.
4. Doodle makes a new friend.
5. Doodle feels different from everyone else.
6. Doodle feels like a failure and needs advice.
7. Doodle takes a challenge and feels victorious.

The prompts above cover common characteristics of giftedness as well as some of the *8 Great Gripes of Gifted Kids* (Galbraith and Delisle): behavior, friendship, bullying, feelings of helplessness about problems in the world, isolation, perfectionism, and challenge.

Planning the Story—Using the Story Board

After you've planted a few seeds, the students use the 2nd graphic organizer, *Doodle Adventure*, to help plan a story. The graphic organizer is good for both language-oriented as well as visually-oriented students because it allows students to plan stories with either pictures, words, or a combination of both.

After students have completed graphic organizers, they should use their work as a visual aid in telling the story to another student. Telling a story to a partner first is similar to writing a rough draft. Let's make sure we do this.

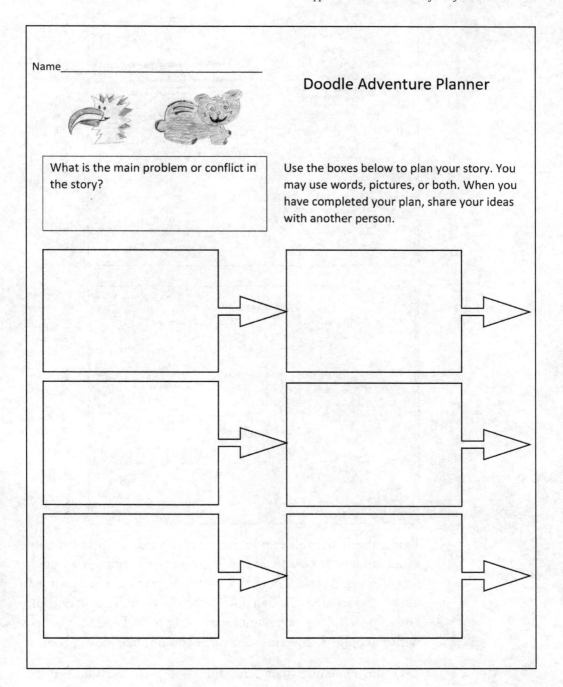

Name______________________________________

Doodle Adventure Planner

What is the main problem or conflict in the story?

Use the boxes below to plan your story. You may use words, pictures, or both. When you have completed your plan, share your ideas with another person.

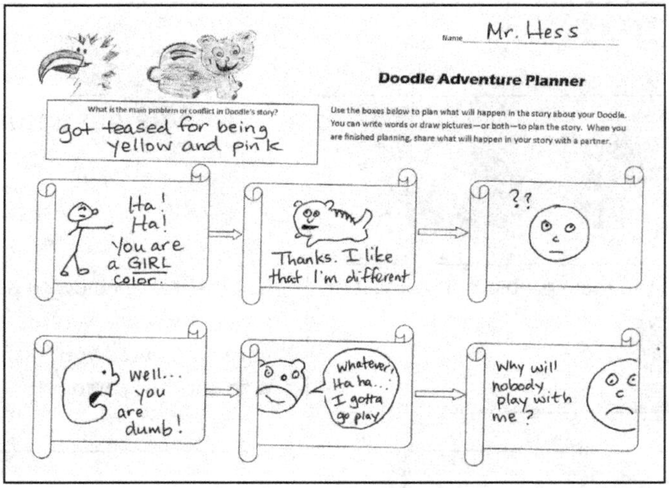

Remember, I stumbled upon this process. I didn't expect so many other students to plan a story about working through a bully's attack or a sticky social situation. In this short space, I had planned a story about being a "tough boy," pride and confidence in oneself, and using self-deprecating humor to shed a bully. I ended the story with the bully discovering that others do not like mean people.

Let's also remember that cartooning is a perfectly valid way to plan a story. Commercials and other short films are often planned in a similar fashion. Let's make sure we aren't requiring a specific number of words. The story on the right was planned by a 2e boy with a CogAT Nonverbal score of 97 but a Verbal score of 27. We honor abilities this way.

Plans, like notecards for public speaking, need only communicate enough information so that the storyteller is able to remember the sequence of events in a story.

Follow-up

My second graders were so amused with their stories (especially those certain boys who think they are comedians and were giggling to themselves during the planning process…you know whom I'm talking about) that they started asking me if they could share their stories with the class before they had even finished. Many spontaneous "story-shares" took place during the planning. It was a lot of fun!

We held off sharing stories until our 3D creations were finished, though. Good thing we did, because one of my students asked, "Can we use our 3D doodle as a puppet when we share our stories?" Of course you can!

Share the stories in any way that works for you. Encourage students to add details to make the stories come to life. Even though it's a bit painful for some kids, it really does help to tell a story aloud in "verbal draft" form to a smaller audience first. Sharing in this way also gives kids ideas about how to enhance their own stories.

I do not require students to share with the entire group if they do not feel comfortable. This is supposed to be a positive experience. Usually such students are willing to share with me. In the future will work on encouraging more confidence…the social-emotional lessons never stop.

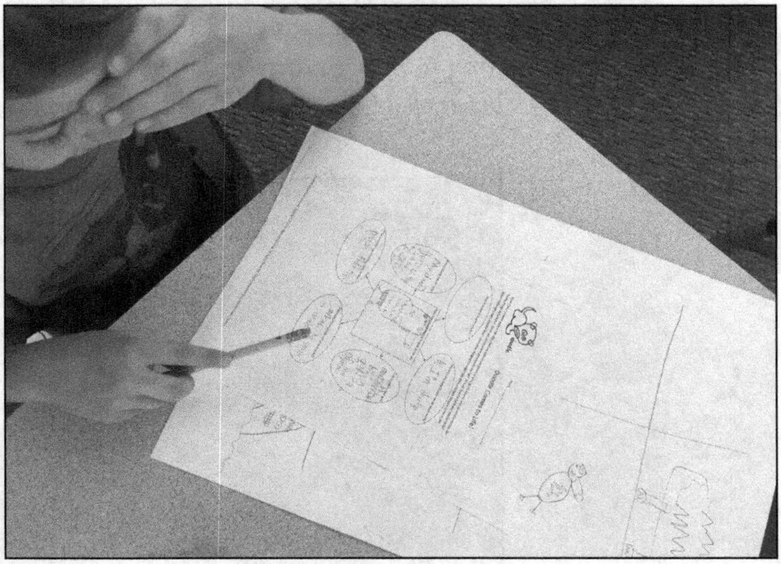

Activity Three: 3D Art

Now we bring our characters into three dimensions. The students really enjoy this activity, and the results create a lively classroom display. I found this to be a more challenging task than I had anticipated because it really does require visual-spatial manipulation and managing multiple perspectives. Once again, this is a great project for your visual-spatial, nonverbal, and ELL kids...but fun for everyone.

1. First, use a full sheet of printer paper to draw and color the doodle character. Emphasize making everything BIG and THICK. Uff...I forgot to do this the first time through, and I had many thin little legs and arms and tails that just would not work for this part! The doodle below is going to be nice and big and thick and easy to cut and stuff with tissue to make it full-bodied and three dimensional.

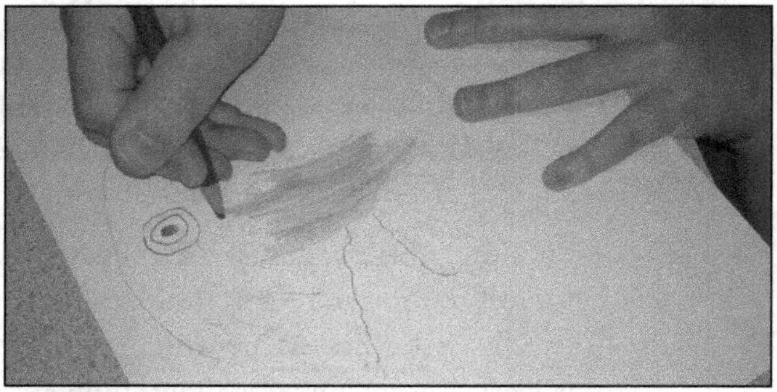

2. Some of the original doodles must be transformed so they can be made three-dimensional. The original giraffe doodle below must be made into a giraffe profile portrait. The thin legs and long neck wouldn't work very well. It's OK. This is how we learn to adjust and edit—just like we do with good writing.

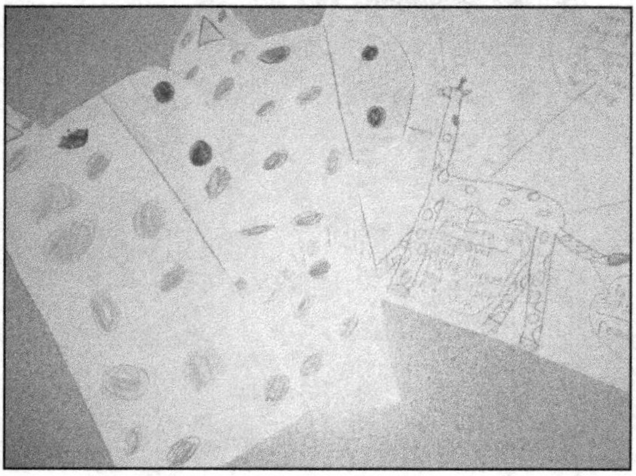

3. Next, tape another sheet of printer paper behind the picture. This is a very handy way to save some time and produce an accurate "backside" to the 3D doodle.

4. Cut out the character's picture (students are cutting through two sheets of paper now).

5. Color the back side (or in some cases, the opposite profile) of the character. Oops…that giraffe above has each half colored on the same sides, but here lies an important editing lesson as a result.

6. Creating the two halves is another opportunity for the students to use their sense of humor for creative elaboration. Watch as some of your more creative students add unexpected details to the back side or reverse profile. The student's elf (next page) is an excellent example of the front/back perspective-taking. A couple parts of the elf were very thin, but since I knew she was an excellent artist, I let her go ahead because I was confident she could make it all work. Later, she will add cotton balls to the hat.

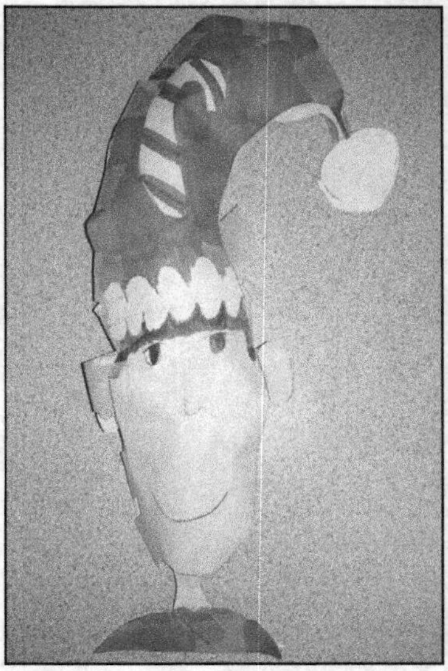

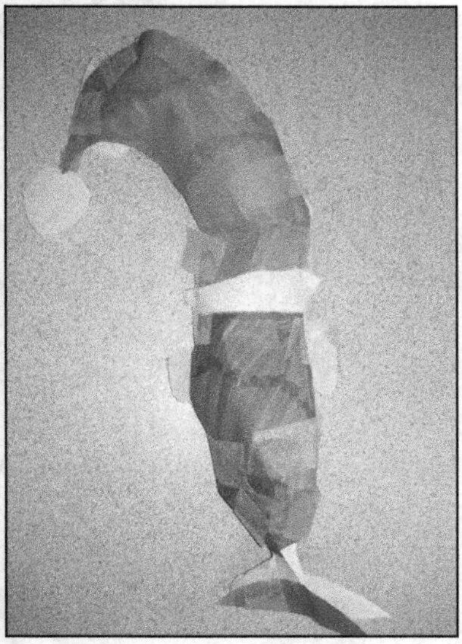

7. Since we're now working in 3D, students might want to add buttons or lace, etc. to their doodles.

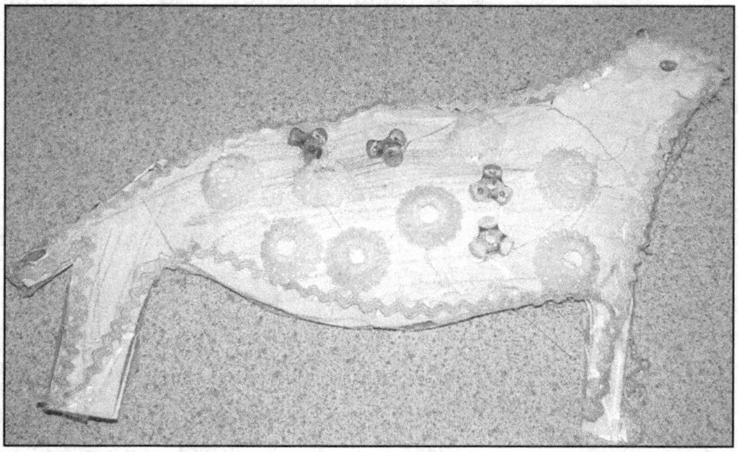

8. Tape around the edges of the two halves of the doodle character, leaving an opening to "stuff" the doodle character with tissues. Voilà! 3D art!

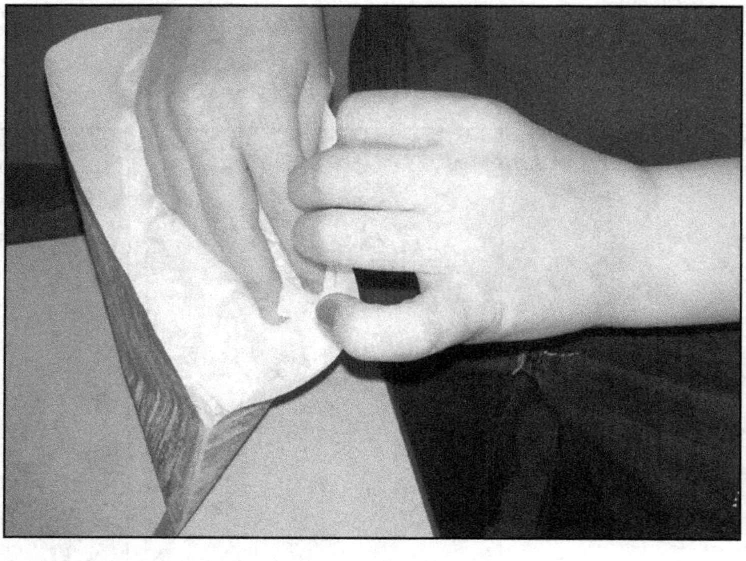

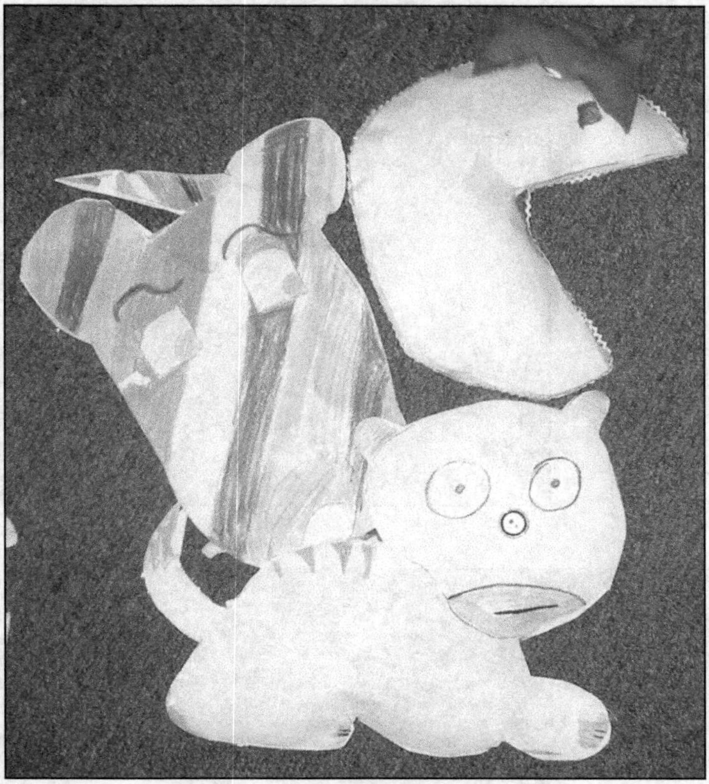

Some students may not feel confident with their artwork. An alternative is to print a large picture from the web and "stuff" it to make it three dimensional. Students will need to be adept at computer and internet skills for this alternative, and because of this, it's a good learning experience as well.

Let's keep in mind that the creativity and artwork are only a part of this unit. Our social-emotional understandings and storytelling work in tandem to move us and challenge us as well.

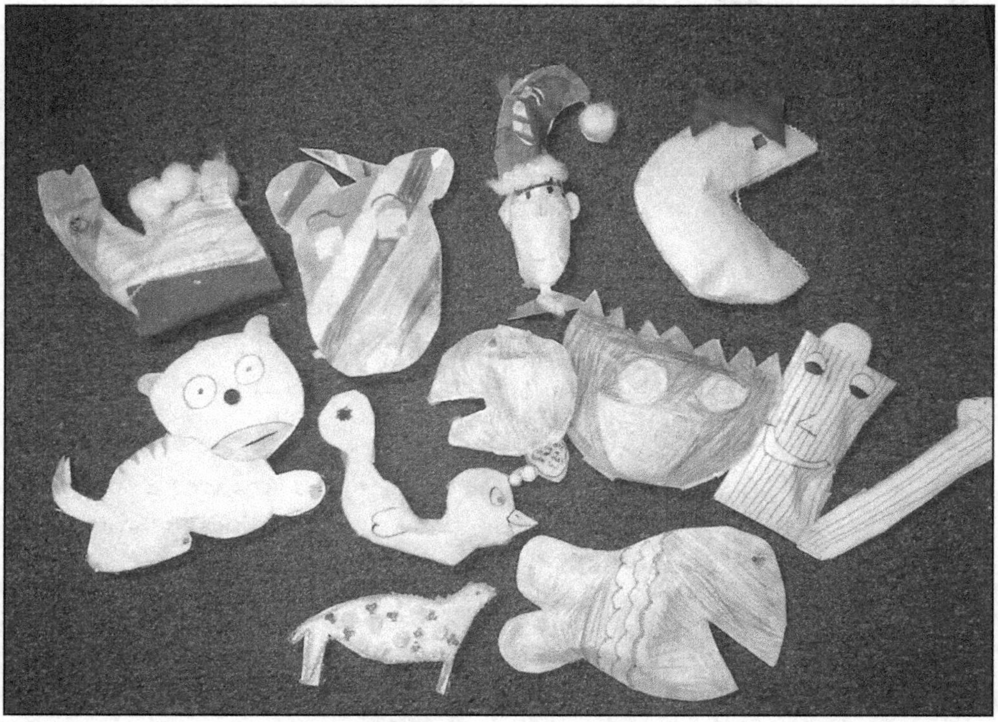

Wrapping Up

Here's a fun improvisational activity. In a future class after completing the Doodles lesson, ask students to share what their Doodle has been up to lately. Gifted kids are blessed with an ability to elaborate and sometimes create whole worlds in their imagination. Enjoy! You will hear some wonderfully creative answers.

Elementary and Middle School GATE

Film Noir

Project, Reading, Writing, Creativity

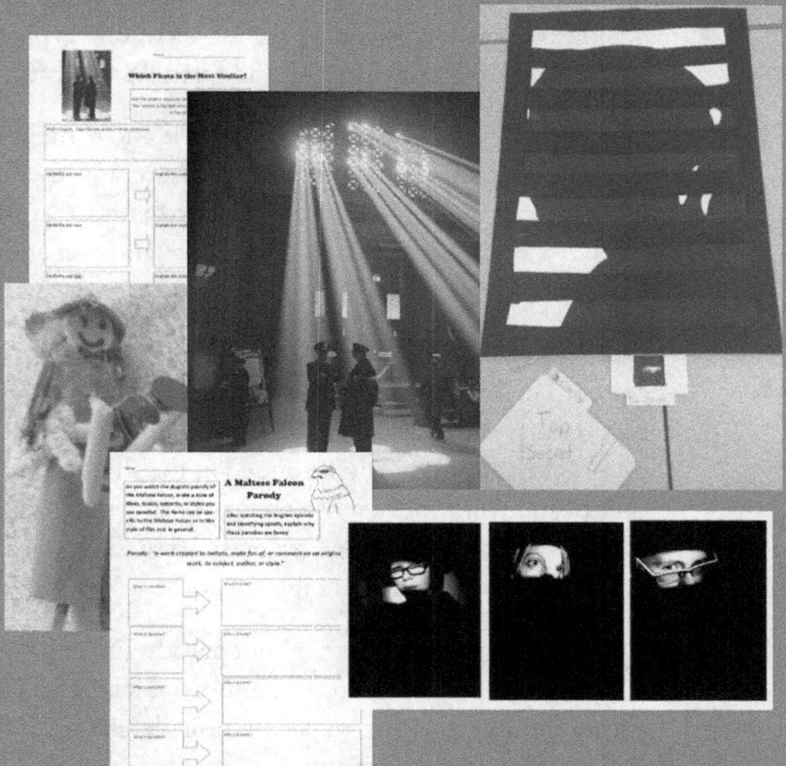

Film Noir

Think. Reflect. Analyze. Explain. Demonstrate.
Be productive, and have fun!

Time: about 6 or 7 hours
Level: 4th-8th Gifted and Talented
Cost of Project: 5 cents per student

Included here are explanations, links to resources, student samples, templates, ready-to-print activity sheets, and applicable standards. Most of the materials required to complete the project are commonly found in the classroom. You'll be ready to start teaching this tomorrow.

Noir in Photography: Students analyze primary source photos in small group and class discussions. This activity contains extension ideas which might be used to further challenge students. Students demonstrate an understanding of tone and mood in photos through the use of a graphic organizer and additional primary source photos.

Film Noir: Students learn about the style and content of film noir through an informative piece of literature and then respond in writing to an interpretive question. Furthermore, students watch videos to learn about specific noir film techniques and then apply what they know to actual vintage trailers of noir films.

Building a Noir Mystery: This is the heart of the unit! We're going to make a mystery poster for a hallway display. The goal is for classmates to figure out the identity of their classmate whose silhouette is mysteriously shrouded in the shadows on the poster. Our poster will feature written clues in a "case file," a mysterious shadowed silhouette set against even more shadows, and an extra *secret* clue featuring an "eyelight" photo.

Noir Parody: Students learn about parody and apply their understanding to a *Rugrats* cartoon episode which spoofs *The Maltese Falcon*. Students support specific noir details from the episode with written explanations.

Hidden Detectives: Students create clothespin detectives, villains, or glamorous and mysterious women in another mystery adventure for the rest of the class. It's a variation on the old "hide the thimble" game—with a written twist.

Noir in Photography

In this activity, students make inferences about a black and white photo and support them with relevant explanations and details. This analytical activity might very well engage our greatest goal as teachers of advanced ability students.

Note: The following photo may be located online at the United States Library of Congress Prints and Photographs Division—an amazing online repository of photos.

We'll build our own definition of noir in this way and make that definition personal and meaningful. Not only is gathering new information through inferences a great approach for gifted learners, it's also an excellent exercise in the use of primary sources.

Think, observe, infer and explain: this process is at the heart of academia.

Key components of noir to take away from the photo below:

- contrast between light and dark
- somber and dark mood, yet passion and energy are contained within
- black and white
- shadows

Although we might require students to write their responses, let's use these questions to generate a lively classroom discussion. The synergy created will give us a strong start in defining "noir," and the students will be invited to reflect through writing in a future activity.

Standards Referenced in this Lesson

CCSS.ELA-LITERACY.SL.5.1

Engage effectively in a range of collaborative discussions (one-on-one, in groups, and teacher-led) with diverse partners on *grade 5 topics and texts*, building on others' ideas and expressing their own clearly.

CCSS.ELA-LITERACY.SL.5.1.C

Pose and respond to specific questions by making comments that contribute to the discussion and elaborate on the remarks of others.

CCSS.ELA-LITERACY.SL.5.1.D

Review the key ideas expressed and draw conclusions in light of information and knowledge gained from the discussions.

CCSS.ELA-LITERACY.RH.6-8.2

Determine the central ideas or information of a primary or secondary source; provide an accurate summary of the source distinct from prior knowledge or opinions.

Photo by Jack Delano, 1943, United States Library of Congress, Prints and Photographs Division

- ❍ List details you see in this photo. Do not make inferences yet.
- ❍ In what sort of building is the photo taken? Use details to support your opinion.
- ❍ What does the posture of the policemen tell us about them and what they might be saying? Use inferences and details to support your opinion.
- ❍ What does the posture of the three women on the bench tell us about them? Use details to support your inference.
- ❍ Many people would find this photo artistically pleasing and even frame it to hang in their home. What is "cool" about this photo?
- ❍ Would this photo be more interesting if it were in color? Support your answer with explanations. Use details to clarify your opinion.
- ❍ What is the mood—the general feeling—of this photo? Explain your choice.
- ❍ What is a good title for this photo?

Sample Responses

Answers will vary—and should! It's important to support inferences and opinions with details.

- List details you see in this photo. Do not make inferences yet.

  Beams of sunlight are coming through high, patterned windows. The beams illuminate the floor. There are many shadows and dark areas in the photo. Three men are wearing uniforms. Two uniforms appear to have badges. People are sitting on long benches. Some are walking or standing. The building's ceiling is high. There is a sign on the left and illuminated letters for a sign in the background.

- In what sort of building is the photo taken? Use details to support your opinion.

  Because of the high ceilings and long benches, this looks like an indoor waiting area. This may be a train station or bus station. Since it is 1943, it is probably not an airport. People look like they are chatting, reading, or just waiting and people watching—all common activities in a station. There might be policemen or security assigned to duty in the station. Maybe the man in the uniform on the left is a valet of some sort, or maybe a policeman. The illuminated sign might be giving directions to travelers, and the sign on the left might be a deli or snack bar menu or a public announcement of some sort.

- What does the posture of the policemen tell us about them and what they might be saying? Use inferences and details to support your opinion.

  They are standing tall but they also seem to be at ease and having a conversation with one another. Nothing is making them suspicious, but their upright posture makes them appear like they are in control of the situation and on the alert as well. They seem like they are having an informal conversation, "See any trouble today? How are the wife and kids?"

- What does the posture of the three women on the bench tell us about them? Use details to support your inference.

  They know each other and they are showing interest in the conversation. The two women on the ends are turned toward the woman in the middle—showing interest and engagement in what is being said. The woman in the middle appears to be wondering about something. She is thoughtful with her hand to her chin.

❍ Many people would find this photo artistically pleasing and even frame it to hang in their home. What is "cool" about this photo?

It's so cool the way the sunlight casts "spotlights" onto the floor and the policemen are standing right in the spotlight. With the rest of the room so much in shadows, the people on the first bench and the policemen really stand out—sort of like popping out of the picture. You wonder what stories they have to tell. We can almost feel what it is like to be there.

❍ Would this photo be more interesting if it were in color? Support your answer with explanations. Use details to clarify your opinion.

No way! The black and white really accentuates the sunlight cutting through the shadows and makes the rest of the photo sort of mysterious. It might be interesting to see the color of clothing people were wearing in 1943. Sometimes it's hard to imagine how colorful the world was before color photography.

❍ What is the mood—the general feeling—of this photo? Explain your choice.

Mysterious and somber or quiet—yet passionate and energetic. The shadows create mystery and a somber mood. It may be a loud and bustling station, but somehow the photo makes it feel quiet and thoughtful. Those beams of light and high ceiling look a lot like stained glass in a church. The long benches even look like church pews. This helps create the somber mood. But look at the way the light cuts through everything with power and passion…sort of like a wonderful energy or beauty or illumination that shows through, connects, and watches over everything.

❍ What is a good title for this photo?

Life Illuminated? Insight into the Darkness? Waiting? Bursting Forth? Spirit? Connection?

The actual title in the Library of Congress archives is *Chicago Illinois, In the Waiting Room at the Union Station.*

Gotta love these kids we teach! Before I had even gotten to the second question, a 5th grade girl came up to me and told me she felt there was a mysterious mood to the picture. It reminded her of a detective story. She had already written ¾ of a page of the story she imagined! Would I like to see it?

I just have to shake my head in happy wonder. She was not only an hour ahead of us in the lesson, but she she had already extended the lesson for her own enjoyment.

Here was an opportunity to let "natural differentiation" occur. I let her work quietly on the story for the rest of the time and then share it with the class at the end of the day. Who wins? Everyone wins.

The next day she came to class with an illustration for her story—very noir and very cool.

Bonus Extension Activities and Assignments:

1. Write or act out the conversation between the policemen.
2. Write or act out the conversation between the ladies.
3. Write or act the thoughts of one of the men on the bench.
4. Pretend you are the photographer, Frank Delano, and explain why you are proud of this picture.
5. Choose music to capture the mood or tone of this photo.

Here is another example of gifted and talented kids dying to express themselves. We were short on time, so I didn't even mention the extension activities listed above. However, two girls came up to me and told me they had a little performance for the class. Could they share? Heck, yes! They acted out the parts of the policemen because I had just mentioned that we could make a guess at what the policemen were saying based on their postures. What a treat for a GATE teacher and for the class!

Let's explore our musical ability with #5. Music, the poetry of mood and interpretation, and fine art come together.

Noir in Photography 2

Use the four photos below and answer this question:

> Which of these four photos would serve as the best companion for *In the Waiting Room at the Union Station*, Chicago, by Frank Delano?
>
> Choose the photo that best corresponds to Delano's style and the mood created.

Students then complete the comparison/explanation graphic organizer further below. This will force the students to reflect upon and summarize the observations they've previously made through class discussion. A sample response is provided further below.

The photos will be more effective if you can project them onto a screen or upload them onto personal devices or computers for viewing. Unfortunately, some quality will be lost if the photos are projected.

There are no clear right or wrong answers—though the two photos on the left are better choices than the two on the right. Hopefully students will focus on the use of shadows and the somber yet powerful tone created through illumination from above.

Standards Referenced in this Lesson

CCSS.ELA-LITERACY.W.5.8

Recall relevant information from experiences or gather relevant information from print and digital sources; summarize or paraphrase information in notes and finished work, and provide a list of sources.

United States Library of Congress Photos, clockwise from top-left: Stanley Kubrick, 1949; Harris and Ewing, 1929; Gordon Parks, 1942; Gordon Parks, 1942

For larger versions of the photos, visit the Library of Congress online.

Name_______________________________

Which Photo is the Most Similar?

Use the graphic organizer below to help explain which of the four photos is the best companion for "In the Waiting Room at the Union Station."

Photo Chosen. Describe the photo in three sentences:

Similarity you see: → **Explain the similarity in one or two sentences:**

Similarity you see: → **Explain the similarity in one or two sentences:**

Similarity you <u>feel</u>: → **Explain the similarity in one or two sentences:**

Name__**SAMPLE RESPONSE**________

Which Photo is the Most Similar?

Use the graphic organizer below to help explain which of the four photos is the best companion for "In the Waiting Room at the Union Station."

Photo Chosen. Describe the photo in three sentences:

A crowd stands waiting. Their faces are illuminated from a light above. We cannot see the people clearly because their bodies are wrapped in dark shadows.

Similarity you see:		Explain the similarity in one or two sentences:
Similarity you see: Light from above.	⇒	**Explain the similarity in one or two sentences:** Both pictures show light coming from above. It's a bright light that pierces the darkness.
Similarity you see: People in shadows.	⇒	**Explain the similarity in one or two sentences:** Both pictures are in black and white and feature dark, dark shadows with bright light surrounding them.
Similarity you feel: Mystery and loneliness.	⇒	**Explain the similarity in one or two sentences:** Both pictures are mysterious. We wonder what people are thinking. Somehow many people seem lonely.

Four Corners Follow-up

Do you know *four corners*? *Four corners* is an excellent technique for urging kids to get up and move and discuss in small groups. It's an effective technique to meet speaking and listening standards.

As a follow-up for the "Noir" activity above, students walk to one of the four corners of the room, based on the photo they've chosen as most similar to the Delano photo. In their corners, the group discusses why they've all chosen the same photo. Everyone is responsible for the discussion.

After students return to their seats, ask one person from each corner to explain why their group has chosen a particular photo.

Standard Referenced in this Lesson

CCSS.ELA-LITERACY.SL.5.3

Summarize the points a speaker makes and explain how each claim is supported by reasons and evidence.

Film Noir

Our exploration of film noir begins with the non-fiction reading excerpt below. Students read the excerpt and then answer the interpretive question.

After students have completed the reading and writing exercise, they'll analyze and discuss three short videos before moving on to creative and artistic challenges involving noir techniques.

Standards Referenced in this Lesson

CCSS.ELA-LITERACY.RI.5.1
Quote accurately from a text when explaining what the text says explicitly and when drawing inferences from the text.

CCSS.ELA-LITERACY.W.5.1
Write opinion pieces on topics or texts, supporting a point of view with reasons and information.

Film Noir

Film Noir is a French term describing a certain style of movie-making. *Film noir* is French for *black film*. So what would a style of moviemaking called *film noir* have to do with black? Even though there is some disagreement about how to define the style of filmmaking called *noir*, there are a couple basic points that are usually agreed upon. The basic points involve the content and the style of film noir.

First, let's think about the style of noir. Imagine shadows—lots of shadows! Here is where the *black* comes into play. Film noir is usually shot in black and white. In a noir film, the characters' faces and bodies are often partly in shadows. White walls in the background also tend to be full of shadows. In the background, one might see the horizontal lines of blinds, the outline of a lamp or chair, or almost anything casting a shadow. The viewer can imagine other parts of a room not seen in a noir film because of the shadows that are cast onto walls by objects in the room not seen directly. Sometimes viewers of noir films see the shadow of a character moving instead of the character themselves. Viewers know what is happening because of the movement of the shadow, but the action is not front and center, it is elusive. This movement by shadow technique becomes an interesting an interesting and mysterious effect on our viewing.

In addition to the style, the content of film noir follows a general pattern. Film noir frequently features detectives, dangerous and mysterious "bad guys," and beautiful and mysterious women. Imagine a detective in a long trench coat, a woman in a dress and heels, and a bad guy in a dark coat with the collar turned up. Imagine a mystery to be solved and dangerous situations. Got that in your mind? If you do, you'll be imagining the content of film noir.

The Perfect Fit for Film Noir

Name________________________________

Many have noted that the style of film noir fits perfectly with a detective crime drama. Use an example or quote from the reading to help prove why this is true. Make sure to explain how the example or quote you've chosen proves that the style of film noir fits perfectly with a detective crime drama.

The Perfect Fit for Film Noir

Name **Sample Response**

Many have noted that the style of film noir fits perfectly with a detective crime drama. Use an example or quote from the reading to help prove why this is true. Make sure to explain how the example or quote you've chosen proves that the style of film noir fits perfectly with a detective crime drama.

The style of film noir fits a detective crime drama because of the heavy use of shadows. The reading piece told me to "imagine shadows . . . Lot of shadows!" Nothing says drama or mystery better than shadows. A shadow always blocks out light. A detective has to uncover things that are partly seen. A detective has to reveal what is in the dark. A shadow is just like a mystery in itself. We might be able to figure out what is in a shadow. We might be able to reveal what is not in the light. Maybe we will be surprised. A good detective finds the answers to questions in the shadows and to things unknown. That is why noir style is perfect for a good detective drama.

With our writing task and analysis complete, let's move on to some of the specifics of film noir.

View this 6 ½ minute video about lighting techniques in noir films:

The Basics of Lighting Film Noir

Link: https://www.youtube.com/watch?v=jsmVL7SDp5Y

This video describes technical details, and it's designed for adults interested in film techniques, but that doesn't mean our gifted learners won't understand. Keeping this in mind, let's not worry too much about the vocabulary used. Our kids are masters at understanding ideas and language given a particular context, and they've already encountered film noir in the reading excerpt. After we watch the video through, answer a few questions in a class discussion:

1. It seems as if shadows are the key component to film noir. Explain how this is so.

   The three-point lighting system is designed to produce shadows. Film noir relies on shadows to create contrasts.

2. What are "key light," "fill light," and "back light?"

   Key Light: The brightest and most dominant light in a three-point lighting set-up.

   Fill Light: fills in the shadows left by the key light.

   Back Light: adds outline that separates the subject from the background.

3. What are "cookies?"

   Cookies are cut-out templates placed in front of light sources which produce shadows.

Don't have a way to stream video to your classroom? Does your school block YouTube? I have been using a free YouTube downloader for years (I use 4K Downloader). Capture videos online and download them to a shared drive. It's easy, safe (so far, anyway) and free!

After viewing techniques for lighting in a noir film, let's view two film noir trailers so we can see how this technique is used. Watch the trailer once through, ask the questions which follow, and then watch the trailer again. Follow-up with a class discussion on the questions (answers will vary).

Out of the Past excerpt, 1947

Link: https://www.youtube.com/watch?v=dn8EImlkRV8

1. How do you know this is an example of film noir?
2. Can you identify a time when the action is shown through shadows instead of directly with people?
3. Identify two shadows on the walls and what they might be.
4. How does the music change our feelings about the action?

Standards Referenced in This Lesson

CCSS.ELA-LITERACY.SL.5.1.C

Pose and respond to specific questions by making comments that contribute to the discussion and elaborate on the remarks of others.

CCSS.ELA-LITERACY.SL.5.1.D

Review the key ideas expressed and draw conclusions in light of information and knowledge gained from the discussions.

Nightmare Alley (1947) Trailer

Link: https://www.youtube.com/watch?v=idlYaKQ1yjw

1. How do you know this is an example of film noir?
2. Pay particular attention to the lighting of the actors and actresses' faces. What do you notice about this lighting, and what effect does it have on the viewer?
3. Would this movie be better if it were filmed in color? Explain.

Building a Noir Mystery

In this activity, we use noir film techniques, subjects, and noir style to build a fun little mystery.

Materials

- ❍ Black and white 11 x 14 construction paper
- ❍ Card stock or recycled file folders
- ❍ Templates (provided)
- ❍ Glue
- ❍ String (optional)
- ❍ Flashlight
- ❍ Tape

We're going to make a mystery poster for a hallway display. The goal is for classmates to figure out the identity of their classmate whose silhouette is mysteriously shrouded in the shadows on the poster. Our poster will feature written clues in a "case file," a mysterious shadowed silhouette set against even more shadows, and an extra *secret* clue featuring an "eyelight" photo. Our finished product will look like this:

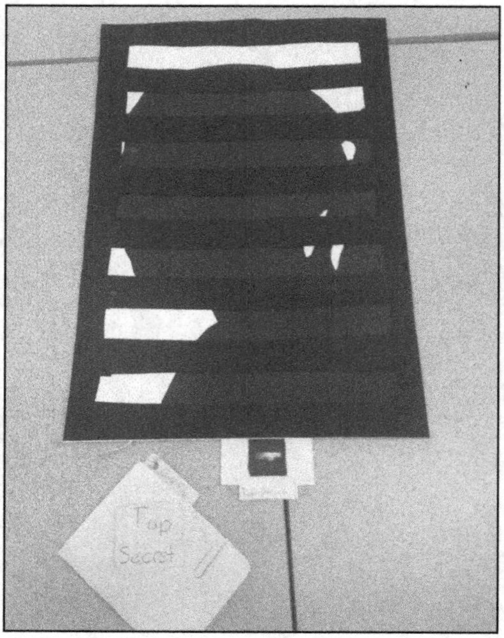

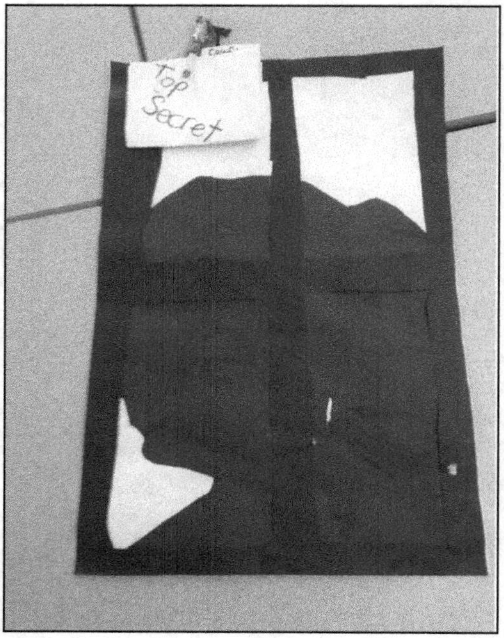

Silhouettes

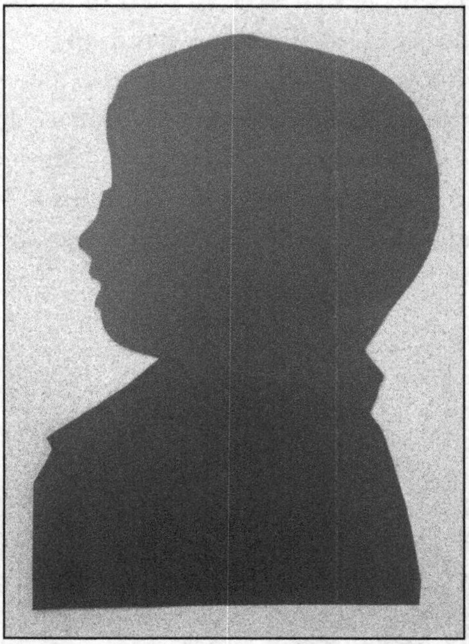

The first thing we'll need is a silhouette of each student in the class. We make the silhouettes by sitting a student in front of black construction paper taped to a wall, shining a flashlight so that a shadow appears on the construction paper, and then tracing the outline of the shadow onto the paper with a red marker.

Tips: I found it much easier, quicker, and more accurate if I did the tracing. I simply called two students at a time into the breakout room next to my classroom and had the students alternate holding the flashlight and sitting for the silhouette. All the other students worked on their case files or "cookies" while we were tracing the silhouettes.

Originally, I thought it would be a good idea to have the students handle all of this themselves in groups of three, but the first group who tried it got next to nothing accomplished in 15 minutes. Regroup. Plan B…

This also might be a good task for a parent volunteer.

Cookies

Each student uses an 11 x 14 sheet of black construction paper to make a "cookie" of window blinds or a window. These will be glued on top of the silhouettes to make a mysterious noir figure. Blinds can be made easily with scissors by folding the paper in half and cutting rectangles as shown. Alternately, students may devise their own window frames. I like how the third one below is a window frame with curtains. It makes me think of The Bates Motel and Psycho.

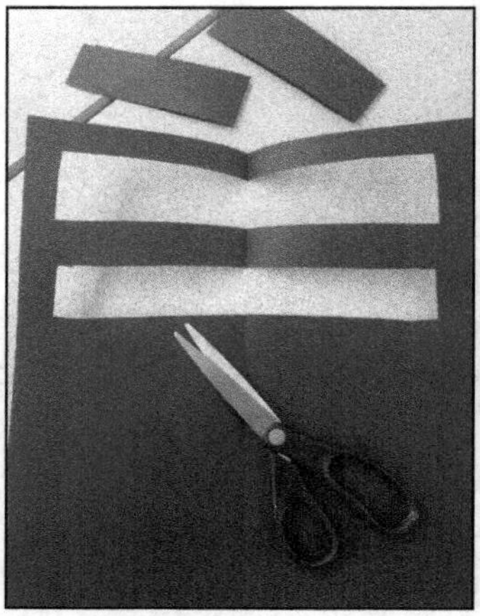

Mini Case File

The *case file* features written clues about the identity of the student on the poster. Use the template below and cardstock or recycled file folders to make a mini file folder.

Students use the template further below to provide clues to the case file. Encourage students to be creative with their responses and to be careful not to give too much away. Don't, for example, choose a nickname as an alias that everyone will know.

Below the templates are sample responses from my class.

We attach the case files to the posters with a bit of string.

Case File Templates

Suspect Also Known As ______________________________

____

Biggest Crime ______________________________

____

Known for ____

____

Known Associates __________________________________

____

Last Known Location______________________________

____

Often Heard Saying ______________________________

____

Photo of Clue Left at Scene of Crime

Suspect Also Known As ______________________________

____

Biggest Crime ______________________________

____

Known for ____

____

Known Associates __________________________________

____

Last Known Location______________________________

____

Often Heard Saying ______________________________

____

Photo of Clue Left at Scene of Crime

Casefile
Top Secret

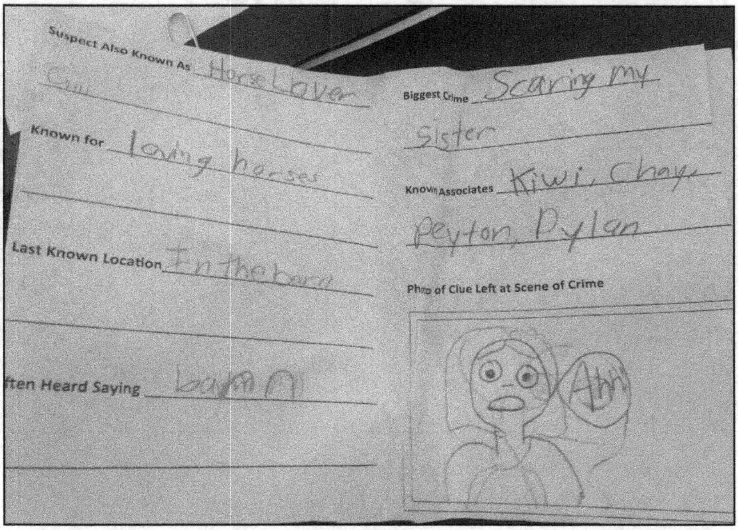
Suspect Also Known As
Horse Lover
Known for
loving horses
Last Known Location
In the barn
ften Heard Saying
Biggest Crime
Scaring my sister
Known Associates
Kiwi, Chay, Peyton, Dylan
Photo of Clue Left at Scene of Crime

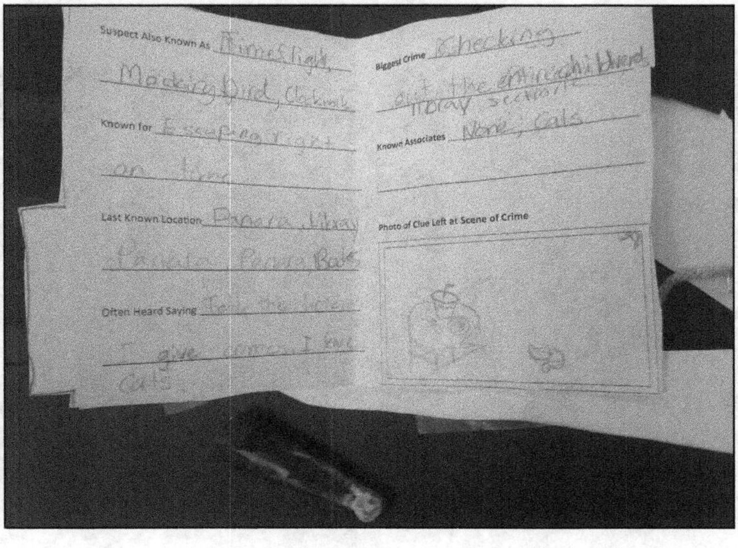
Suspect Also Known As
Known for
Last Known Location
Often Heard Saying
Biggest Crime
Checking
Known Associates
None, Cats
Photo of Clue Left at Scene of Crime

Eyelight Photo

We add one more clue to our posters—a noir "eyelight" photo on a "pull-down" tab at the bottom.

As we know from our study of noir film, our glamorous ladies and heroes often have eyes and brows highlighted. We can create the same effect with a black construction paper "cookie."

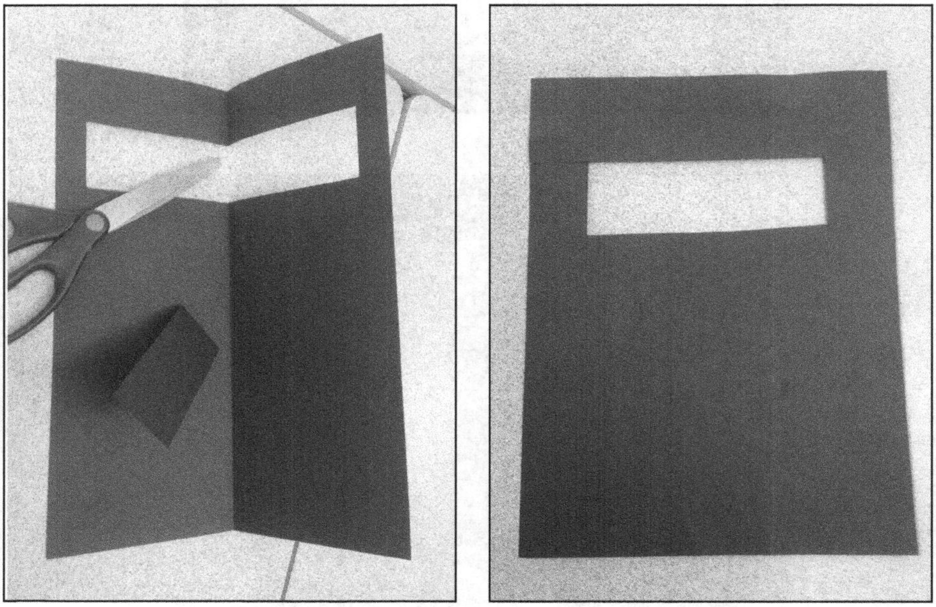

Take a photo of each student using the cookie, a dark room, and a flashlight. We took our photos with an iPad and chose "Noir" on the color choices to produce a really cool effect. Check a few of these out!

We add a very small version (save your printer ink!) to a secret pull-out tab on the bottom of the poster. It's a fun *noirish* clue! We make the pull-out tab with a couple standard notecards and some tape. See the picture below.

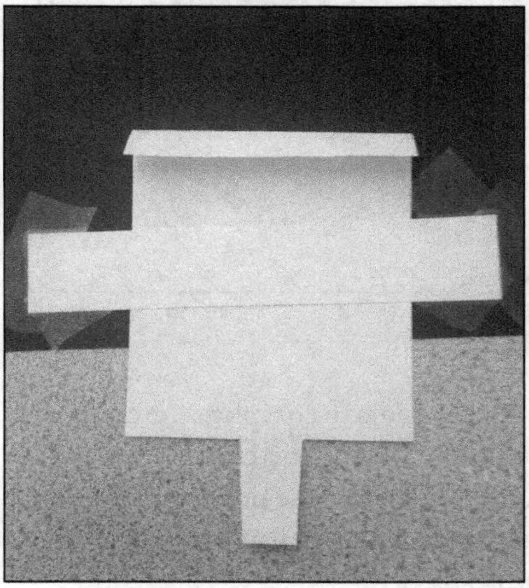

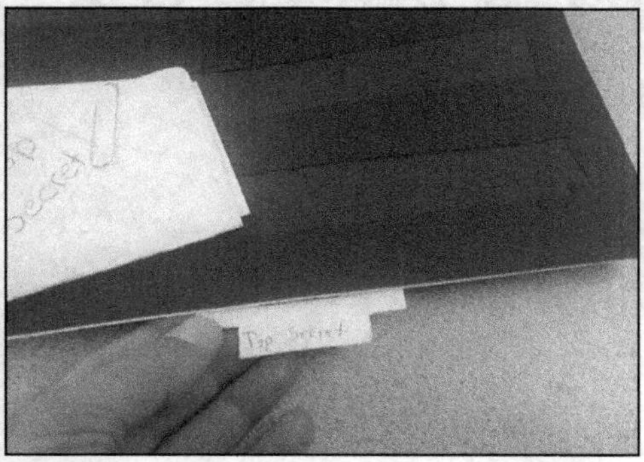

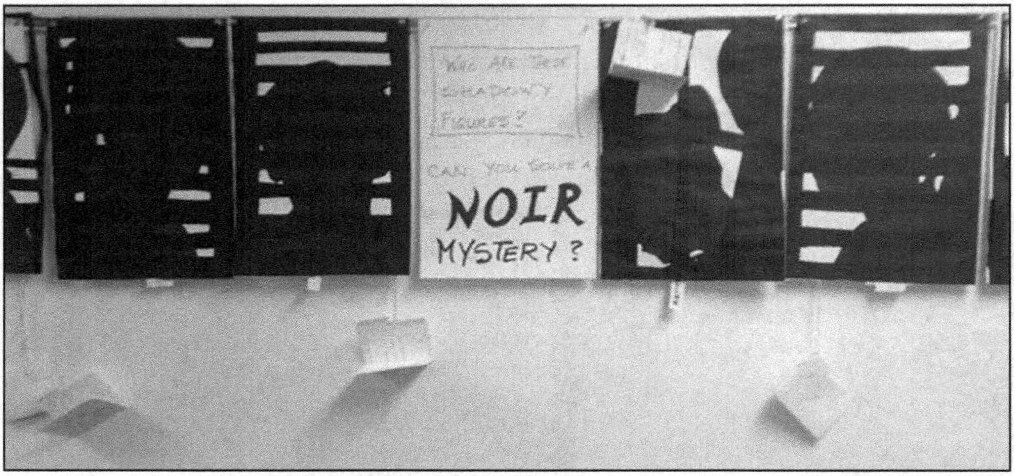

Noir Parody

Our mystery projects take several hours to complete. After we have worked on them for a few hours, I bring the class back together for a lesson on parody before we complete the projects. This allows us to get centered and re-organized—as well as reminded of our purpose—before we move on.

Film noir—with its distinctive style, its glamorous women, and its sullen gumshoes—is an easy target for parodies. Parodies are great fun for gifted kids!

To launch this lesson, show students several images which parody works of art or advertisements. I have not included them here because of potential copyright issues, but typing in "parody" in a Google image search will get you where you need to be. We used parodies of Grant Wood's *American Gothic*, Wyeth's *Nighthawks*, iPod, Pepsi, McDonalds, and Starbucks.

With each parody viewed, ask students what makes the parody funny. After viewing several, ask what the images have in common.

Students should be able to identify a key trait of parodies: they make fun of something we know about. In other words, they're sort of like an inside joke.

With this in mind, take a closer look at the definition of parody, and discuss its meaning with the students.

Parody: a work created to imitate, make fun of, or comment on an original work, its subject, author, or style.

Take a minute to remind students about the key elements of film noir we've discussed. We're about to watch a *Rugrats* noir parody, *Radio Daze*.

Before we watch *Radio Daze*, we'll need a bit of background on one of the most famous noir films—*The Maltese Falcon*.

Maltese Falcon Trailer

Watch the trailer at this link: https://www.youtube.com/watch?v=h7QPtU_qtQ4

Don't worry if you've never seen *The Maltese Falcon* or don't glean more specific knowledge of the movie in the trailer. We only need to know that the movie involves a falcon statue called the Maltese Falcon, that it is a famous film, and that the movie is full of all the classic noir elements.

Rugrats Maltese Falcon Parody

https://www.youtube.com/watch?v=HBA-IanV2RE

While students watch, they should complete the left side of the activity sheet below. Stop the video near the beginning and complete the first part of the graphic organizer together.

After viewing the full parody, complete the activity sheet.

Share completed responses with the class. After students have shared responses, ask this key question (answers will vary):

"Can a parody be funny if we don't know the original source, style, subject, or author?"

Name________________________________

A Maltese Falcon Parody

As you watch the *Rugrats* parody of the *Maltese Falcon,* make a note of ideas, topics, subjects, or styles you see spoofed. The items can be specific to the *Maltese Falcon* or to the style of film noir in general.

After watching the Rugrats episode and identifying spoofs, explain why these parodies are funny.

Parody: "a work created to imitate, make fun of, or comment on an original work, its subject, author, or style."

What is parodied?	→	Why is it funny?
What is parodied?	→	Why is it funny?
What is parodied?	→	Why is it funny?
What is parodied?	→	Why is it funny?

Name___SAMPLE RESPONSES_____

As you watch the Rugrats parody of the Maltese Falcon, make a note of ideas, topics, subjects, or styles you see spoofed. The items can be specific to the Maltese Falcon or to the style of film noir in general.

A Maltese Falcon Parody

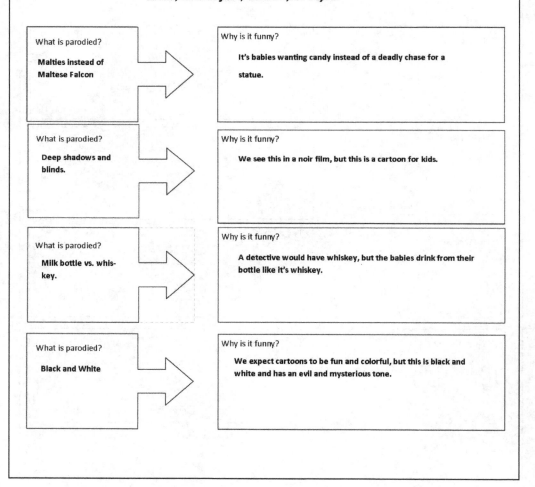

After watching the Rugrats episode and identifying spoofs, explain why these parodies are funny.

Parody: "a work created to imitate, make fun of, or comment on an original work, its subject, author, or style."

What is parodied?

Malties instead of Maltese Falcon

Why is it funny?

It's babies wanting candy instead of a deadly chase for a statue.

What is parodied?

Deep shadows and blinds.

Why is it funny?

We see this in a noir film, but this is a cartoon for kids.

What is parodied?

Milk bottle vs. whiskey.

Why is it funny?

A detective would have whiskey, but the babies drink from their bottle like it's whiskey.

What is parodied?

Black and White

Why is it funny?

We expect cartoons to be fun and colorful, but this is black and white and has an evil and mysterious tone.

Our Final Mystery

Let's finish with some more fun and creativity.

This portion of the lesson is a variation on the old "hide the thimble" game. We use flat 2 ½" clothespins to create our *femme fatales* and detectives.

Students worked at various paces to create their noir mystery posters, and it was good to have this activity for students who finished the poster the quickest.

Start by creating a detective, villain, or glamorous lady with the clothespin. Some of my kids really took off with this—wanting to do more than one, wanting to take home the project, etc. Check them out!

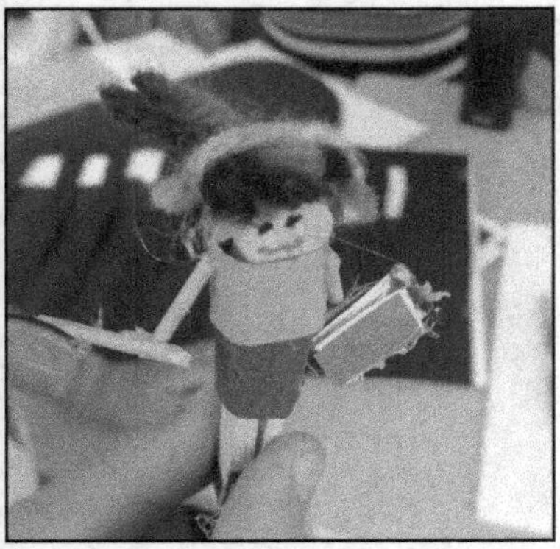

A Carmen San Diego, a school girl detective holding a magnifying glass and notebook, a Miss Marple. I think those femme fatales look pretty cute—not dangerous at all...but does that make them even more dangerous?

Now it's time to hide the clothespin!

Once the clothespin people have been created, students write three or more clues on separate notecards. These clues will point classmates to various parts of the room where they will find additional clues—and eventually—the clothespin. The first notecard is read by the student. It might say something like, "Don't get board with the vocabulary (pun intended)." On the whiteboard at the front of the room, under the sign for this week's vocabulary, the second clue will be taped. This clue will point to another spot in the room, and so on...until all the clues are gathered and the clothespin is found.

My 5th graders loved making and hiding the clues. They loved solving the mysteries too. We completed one or two mysteries every day until we were done. That way students had time to hide their clues, and we had the little mystery to look forward to every day for several days.

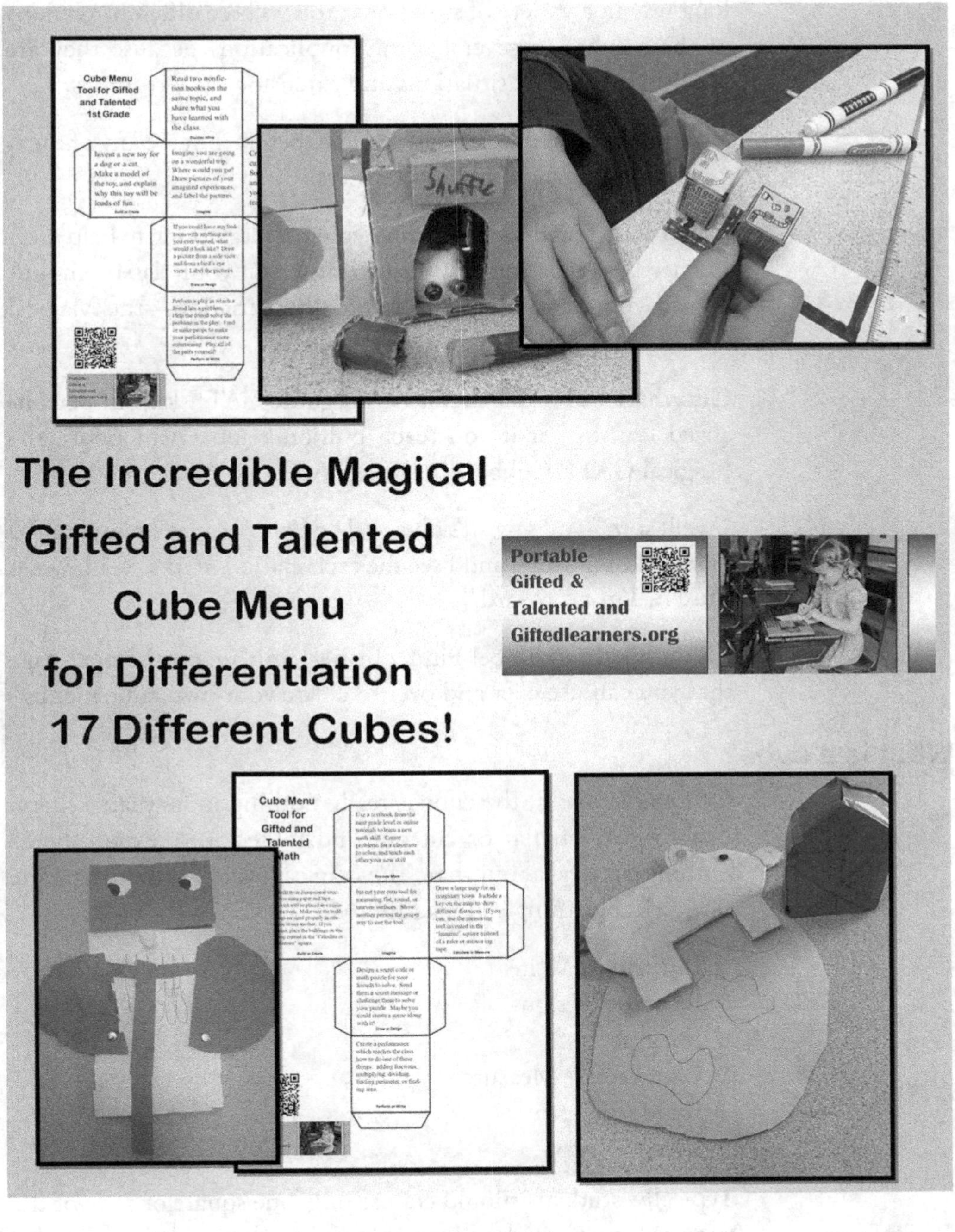
Cube Menu
Tool for Gifted
and Talented
1st Grade
Read two nonfiction books on the same topic, and share what you have learned with the class.
Invent a new toy for a dog or a cat. Make a model of the toy, and explain why this toy will be loads of fun.
Imagine you are going on a wonderful trip. Where would you go? Draw pictures of your imagined experiences, and label the pictures.
Shuffle
The Incredible Magical
Gifted and Talented
Cube Menu
for Differentiation
17 Different Cubes!
Portable
Gifted &
Talented and
Giftedlearners.org
Cube Menu
Tool for
Gifted and
Talented
Math

The Magical GATE Cube works in many ways. It goes a long, long way in a variety of situations. You will see different versions of these cubes in several of my publications because they are applicable to many situations and extension opportunities.

Sure, you've seen differentiation cubes before, but are any of them magical and made for gifted learners?

Classroom Teachers: If you find yourself scrambling to help meet the needs of those rascally gifted learners in your classroom—or even if you are a master at classic differentiation—the Magical GATE Cube will serve you well.

Gifted Resource Teachers: If you guide GATE kids in personalized learning or if you teach pull-outs and talent pools, the Magical GATE Cube will serve you well.

"Well, sure," you say, "it's obviously magic because I see all of the words like amazing, and I see the exclamation marks, but how do I use it? I'm no wizard."

Ahhh, but you will be! Find a blank template on the next page that you can use over and over to create your own cube menus.

What is a *cube*?

On the one hand, the cube is really nothing more than a menu that can be left flat or cut out and folded into a die. There's nothing magical about that. The magical part of the cube are the categorical learning styles addressed:

- ❍ Perform or Write
- ❍ Draw or Design
- ❍ Imagine
- ❍ Calculate or Measure
- ❍ Build or Create
- ❍ Discover More

Typically, students should choose only one square or style of the cube to complete; however, this is not always the case. Judge from the time available as well as the enthusiasm of the students for each cube.

Students might use the cube as a flat menu or tic-tac-toe option. Cubes can be cut and folded into a three-dimensional cube where they are rolled—the option coming to the top being the required task.

Generally, however, it's better to allow the power of student choice.

Cubes address student choice, challenge, and complexity—all fantastic ways to help meet the needs of gifted learners.

A little creativity and classroom variety helps the use of cubes go a long way:

- For gifted learners to go further in depth in a classroom topic.
- For gifted learners to explore topic related to classroom content.
- As a substitute for reviews and extra practice—often redundant for gifted learners
- To engage students with choice and personalized passion projects.

Jigsaw with the Cube

1. Allow students to choose which task they will complete.
2. Students who've chosen the same task collaborate to understand the question and then may choose to collaborate when they complete products; however, each student needs his or her own product.

3. Students share their products with others who have completed different products—essentially teaching other students an aspect of the topic or skill involved.

4. If you choose, have students choose another task from the cube, and complete the jigsaw again. Watch how the products grow and mature!

Personalized Learning

Students might explore a topic further, more in-depth, or with more motivating learning styles.

Let's help this student focus on products by developing a cube based on his or her choice of topics. If you work with advanced learning plans, help the student find an appropriate task which lands in his or her talent area and academic goals. Helping kids express talents is one of the most important aspects of a gifted program.

Cube Menu Tool for Gifted and Talented

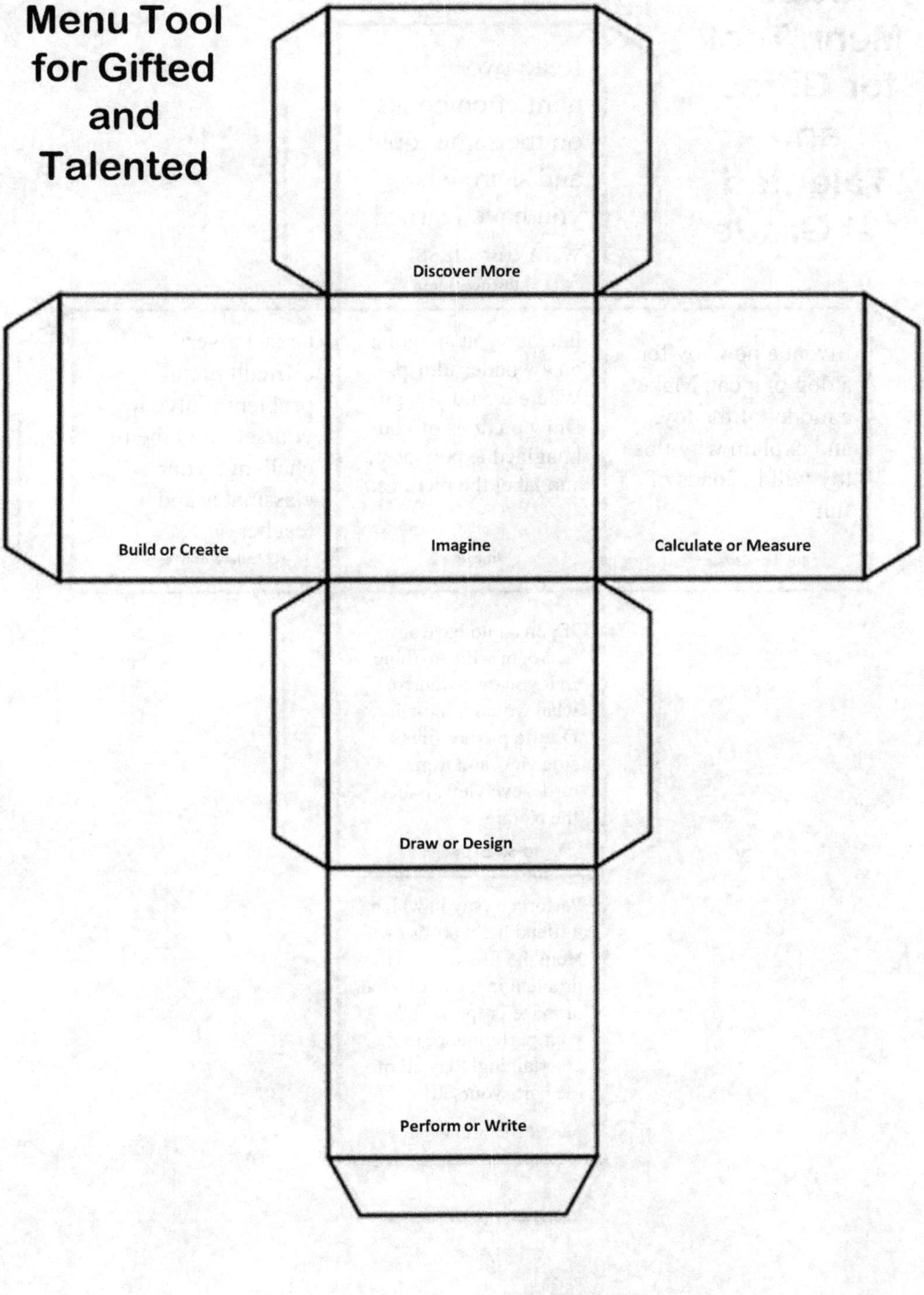

Cube Menu Tool for Gifted and Talented 1st Grade

Read two nonfiction books on the same topic, and share what you have learned with the class.

Discover More

Invent a new toy for a dog or a cat. Make a model of the toy, and explain why this toy will be loads of fun.

Build or Create

Imagine you are going on a wonderful trip. Where would you go? Draw pictures of your imagined experiences, and label the pictures.

Imagine

Create a very difficult math problem. Solve it yourself, and then challenge your classmates and teacher.

Calculate or Measure

If you could have any bedroom with anything in it you ever wanted, what would it look like? Draw a picture from a side view and from a bird's eye view. Label the pictures.

Draw or Design

Perform a play in which a friend has a problem. Help the friend solve the problem in the play. Find or make props to make your performance more entertaining. Play all of the parts yourself!

Perform or Write

Cube Menu Tool for Gifted and Talented Dogs

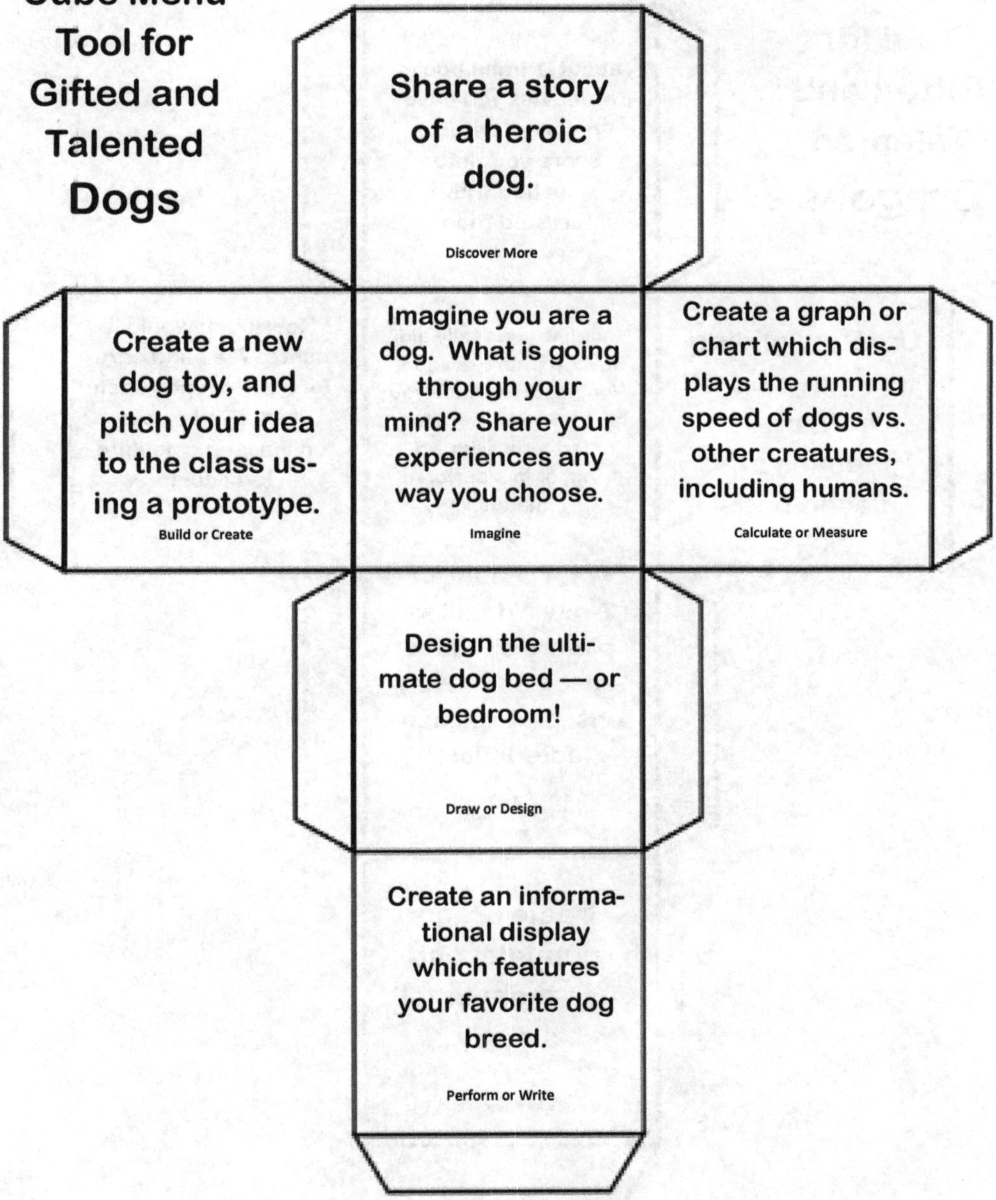

Share a story of a heroic dog.
Discover More
Create a new dog toy, and pitch your idea to the class using a prototype.
Build or Create
Imagine you are a dog. What is going through your mind? Share your experiences any way you choose.
Imagine
Create a graph or chart which displays the running speed of dogs vs. other creatures, including humans.
Calculate or Measure
Design the ultimate dog bed — or bedroom!
Draw or Design
Create an informational display which features your favorite dog breed.
Perform or Write

Cube Menu Tool for Gifted and Talented Dragons

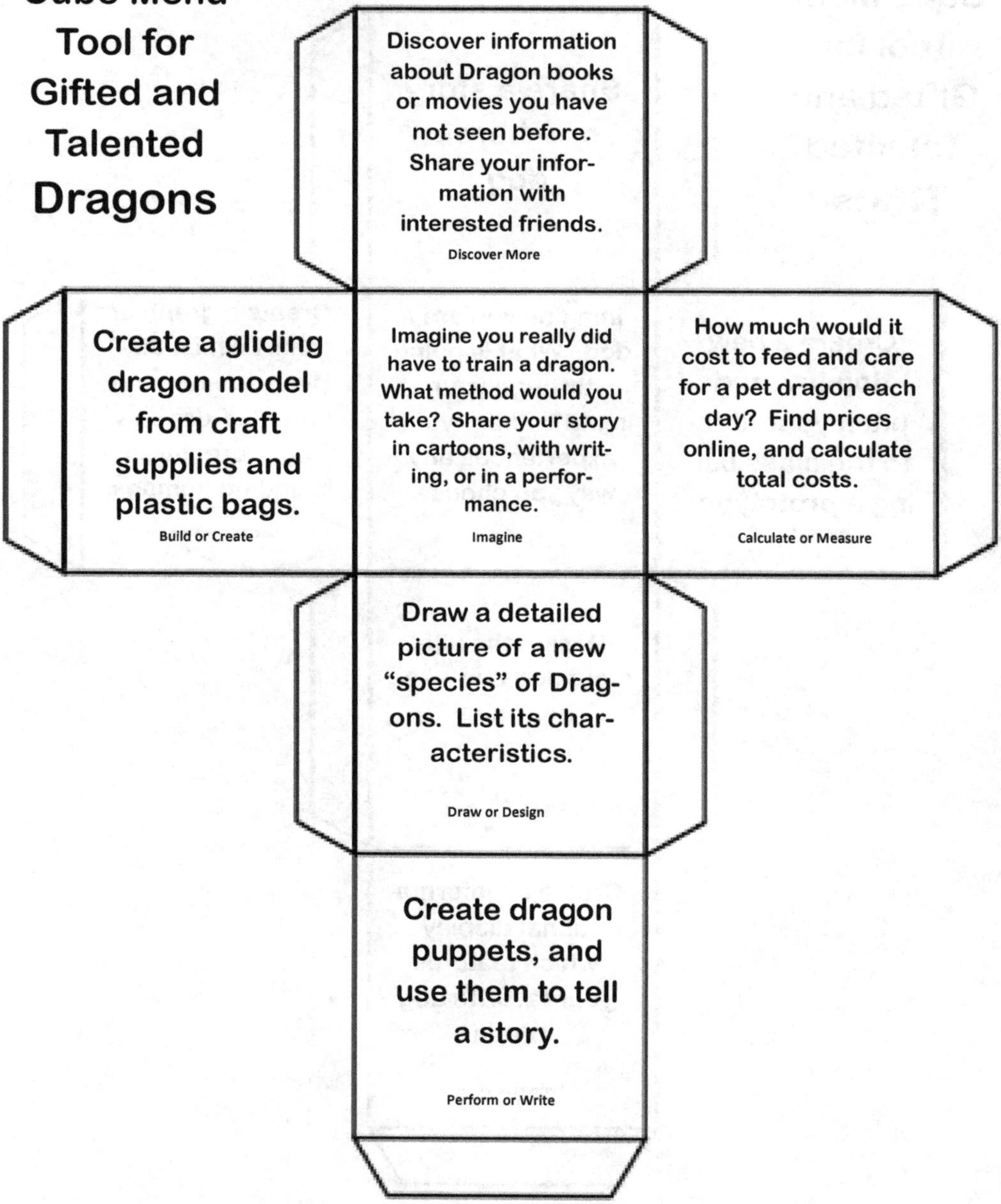
Discover information about Dragon books or movies you have not seen before. Share your information with interested friends.
Discover More
Create a gliding dragon model from craft supplies and plastic bags.
Build or Create
Imagine you really did have to train a dragon. What method would you take? Share your story in cartoons, with writing, or in a performance.
Imagine
How much would it cost to feed and care for a pet dragon each day? Find prices online, and calculate total costs.
Calculate or Measure
Draw a detailed picture of a new "species" of Dragons. List its characteristics.
Draw or Design
Create dragon puppets, and use them to tell a story.
Perform or Write

Cube Menu Tool for Gifted and Talented Flight

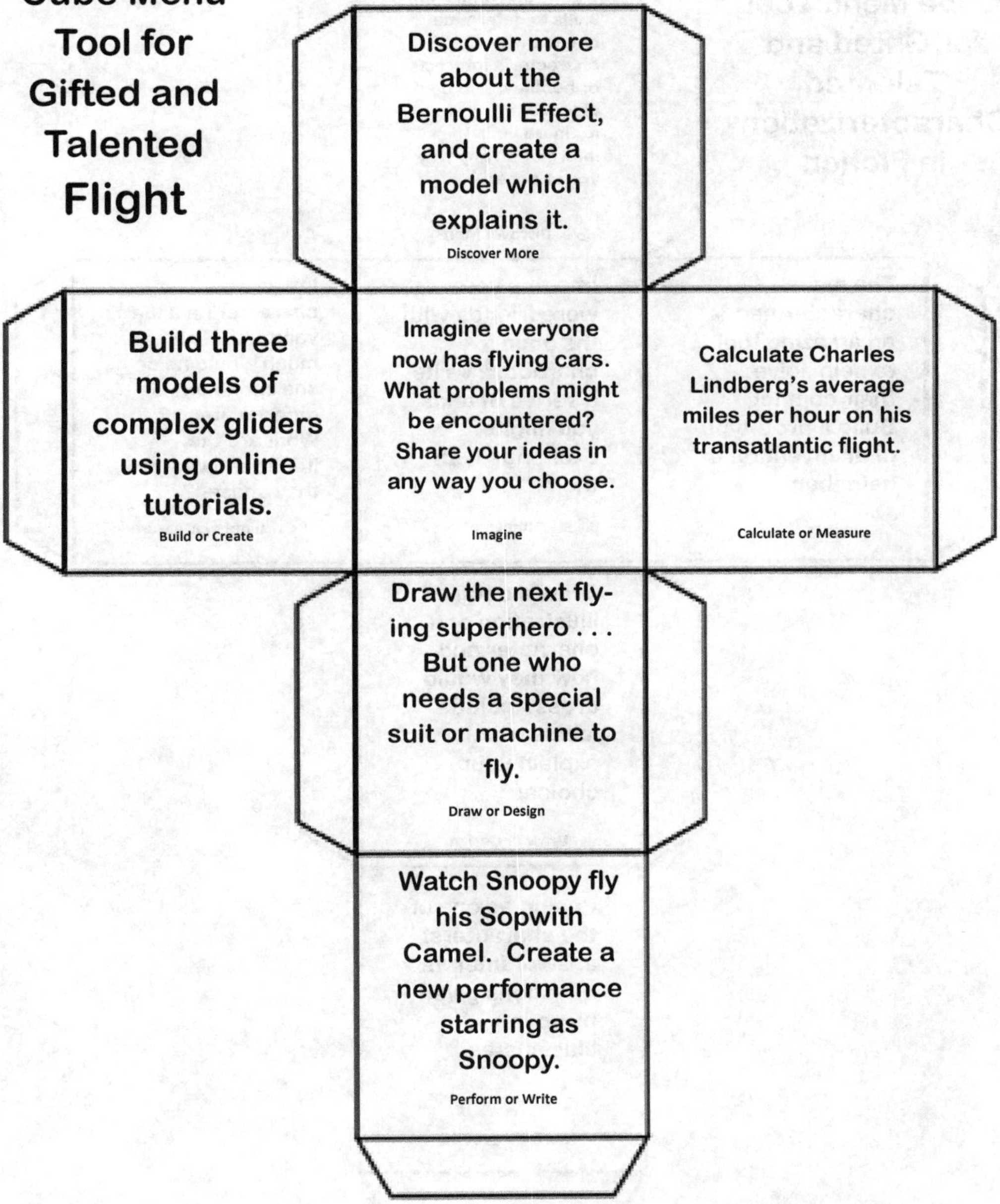

Discover more about the Bernoulli Effect, and create a model which explains it.
Discover More
Build three models of complex gliders using online tutorials.
Build or Create
Imagine everyone now has flying cars. What problems might be encountered? Share your ideas in any way you choose.
Imagine
Calculate Charles Lindberg's average miles per hour on his transatlantic flight.
Calculate or Measure
Draw the next fly-ing superhero . . . But one who needs a special suit or machine to fly.
Draw or Design
Watch Snoopy fly his Sopwith Camel. Create a new performance starring as Snoopy.
Perform or Write

Cube Menu Tool for Gifted and Talented Characterization in Fiction

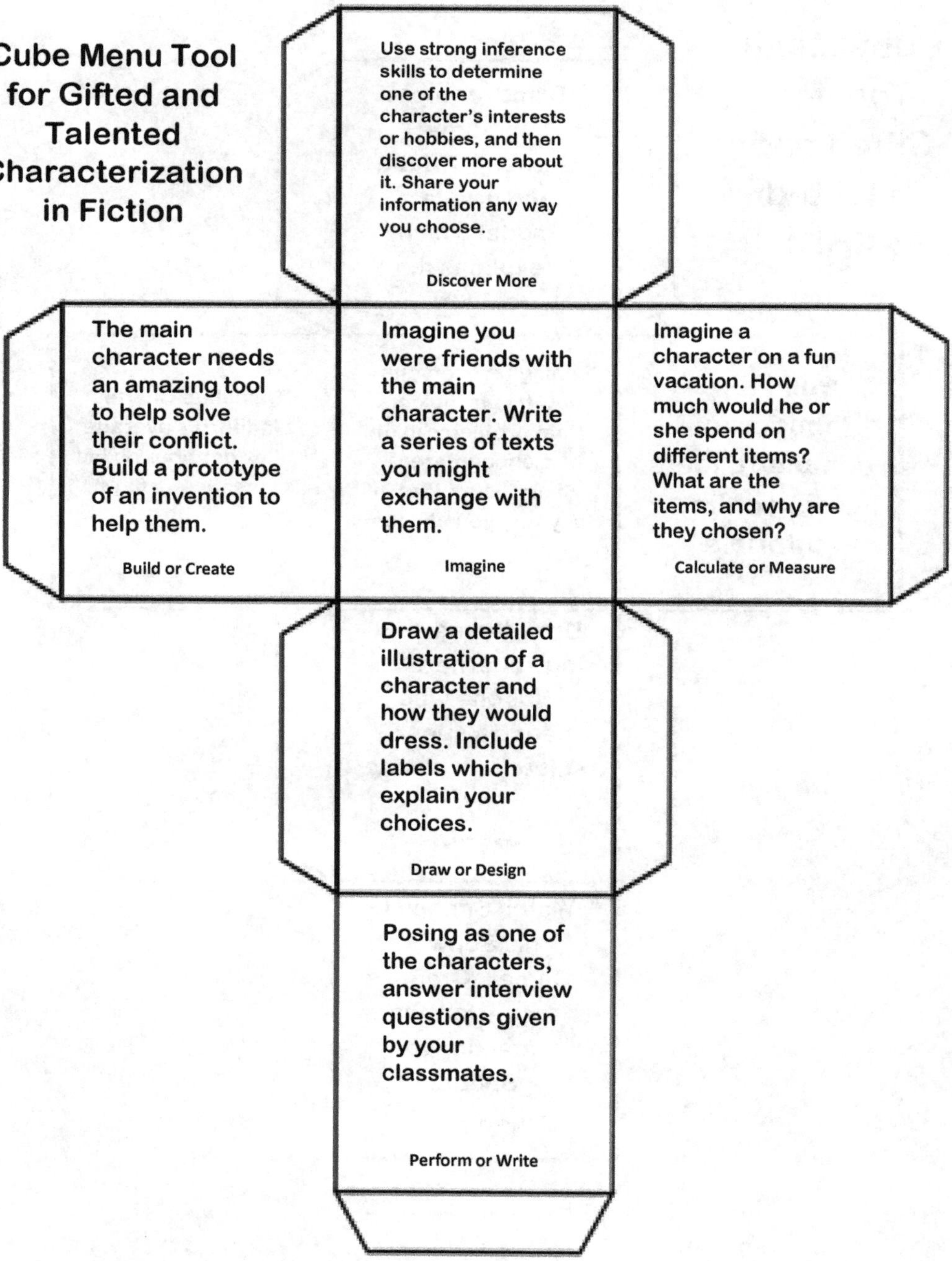

Use strong inference skills to determine one of the character's interests or hobbies, and then discover more about it. Share your information any way you choose.
Discover More
The main character needs an amazing tool to help solve their conflict. Build a prototype of an invention to help them.
Build or Create
Imagine you were friends with the main character. Write a series of texts you might exchange with them.
Imagine
Imagine a character on a fun vacation. How much would he or she spend on different items? What are the items, and why are they chosen?
Calculate or Measure
Draw a detailed illustration of a character and how they would dress. Include labels which explain your choices.
Draw or Design
Posing as one of the characters, answer interview questions given by your classmates.
Perform or Write

Cube Menu Tool for Gifted and Talented Fiction

Setting

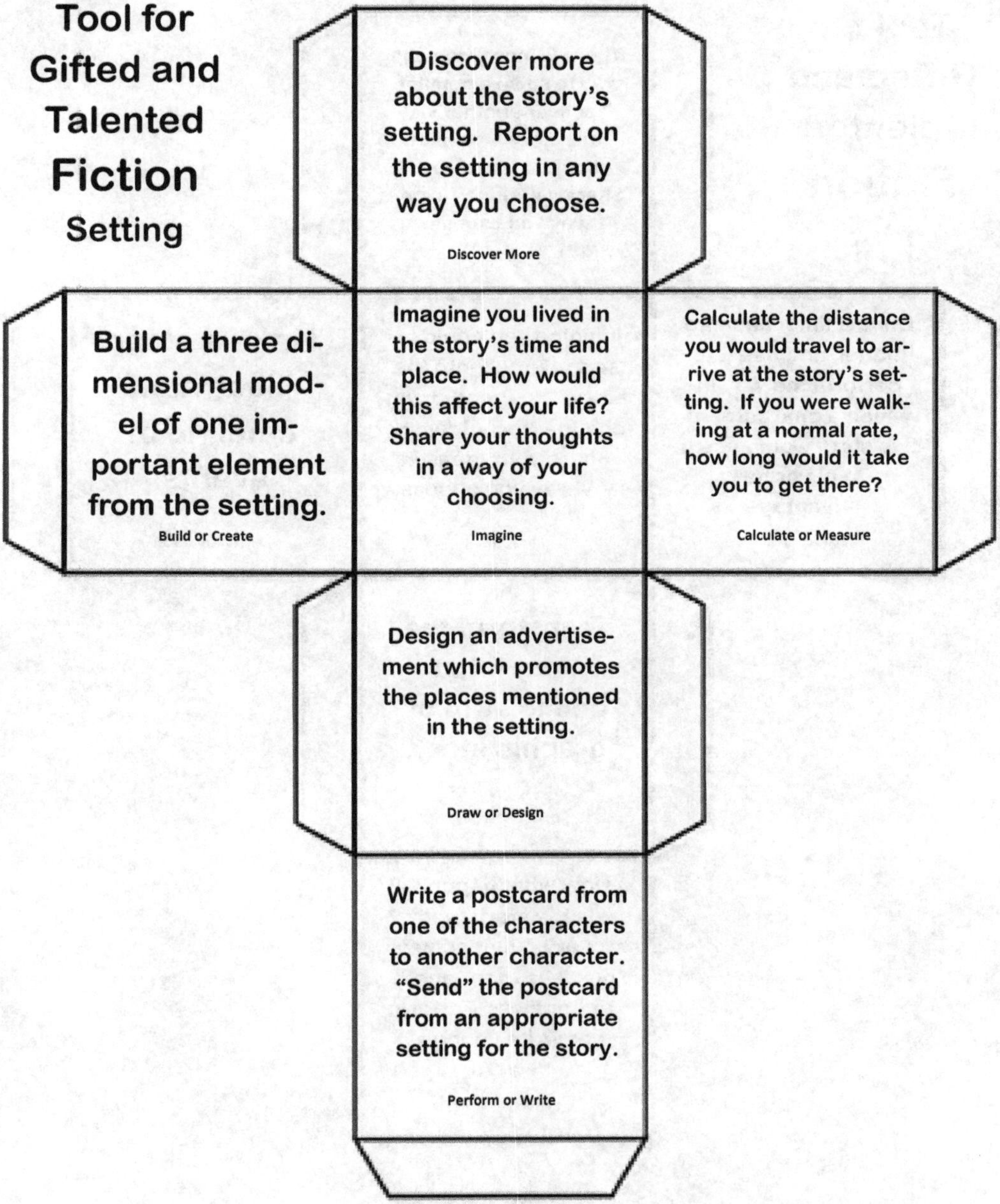

Discover more about the story's setting. Report on the setting in any way you choose.
Discover More
Build a three dimensional model of one important element from the setting.
Build or Create
Imagine you lived in the story's time and place. How would this affect your life? Share your thoughts in a way of your choosing.
Imagine
Calculate the distance you would travel to arrive at the story's setting. If you were walking at a normal rate, how long would it take you to get there?
Calculate or Measure
Design an advertisement which promotes the places mentioned in the setting.
Draw or Design
Write a postcard from one of the characters to another character. "Send" the postcard from an appropriate setting for the story.
Perform or Write

Cube Menu Tool for Gifted and Talented

Fiction

Plot

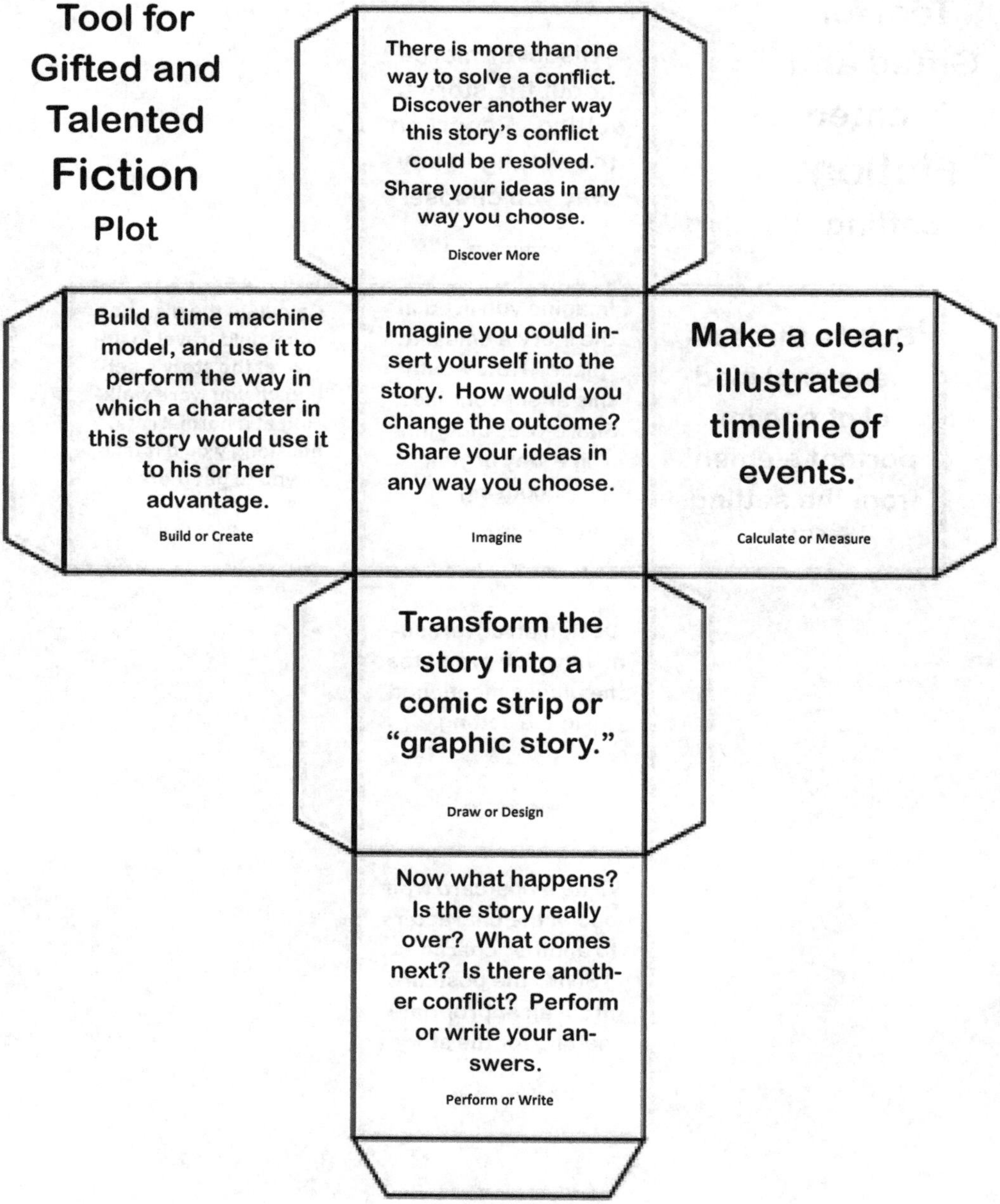

There is more than one way to solve a conflict. Discover another way this story's conflict could be resolved. Share your ideas in any way you choose.
Discover More
Build a time machine model, and use it to perform the way in which a character in this story would use it to his or her advantage.
Build or Create
Imagine you could insert yourself into the story. How would you change the outcome? Share your ideas in any way you choose.
Imagine
Make a clear, illustrated timeline of events.
Calculate or Measure
Transform the story into a comic strip or "graphic story."
Draw or Design
Now what happens? Is the story really over? What comes next? Is there another conflict? Perform or write your answers.
Perform or Write

Cube Menu Tool for Gifted and Talented Horses

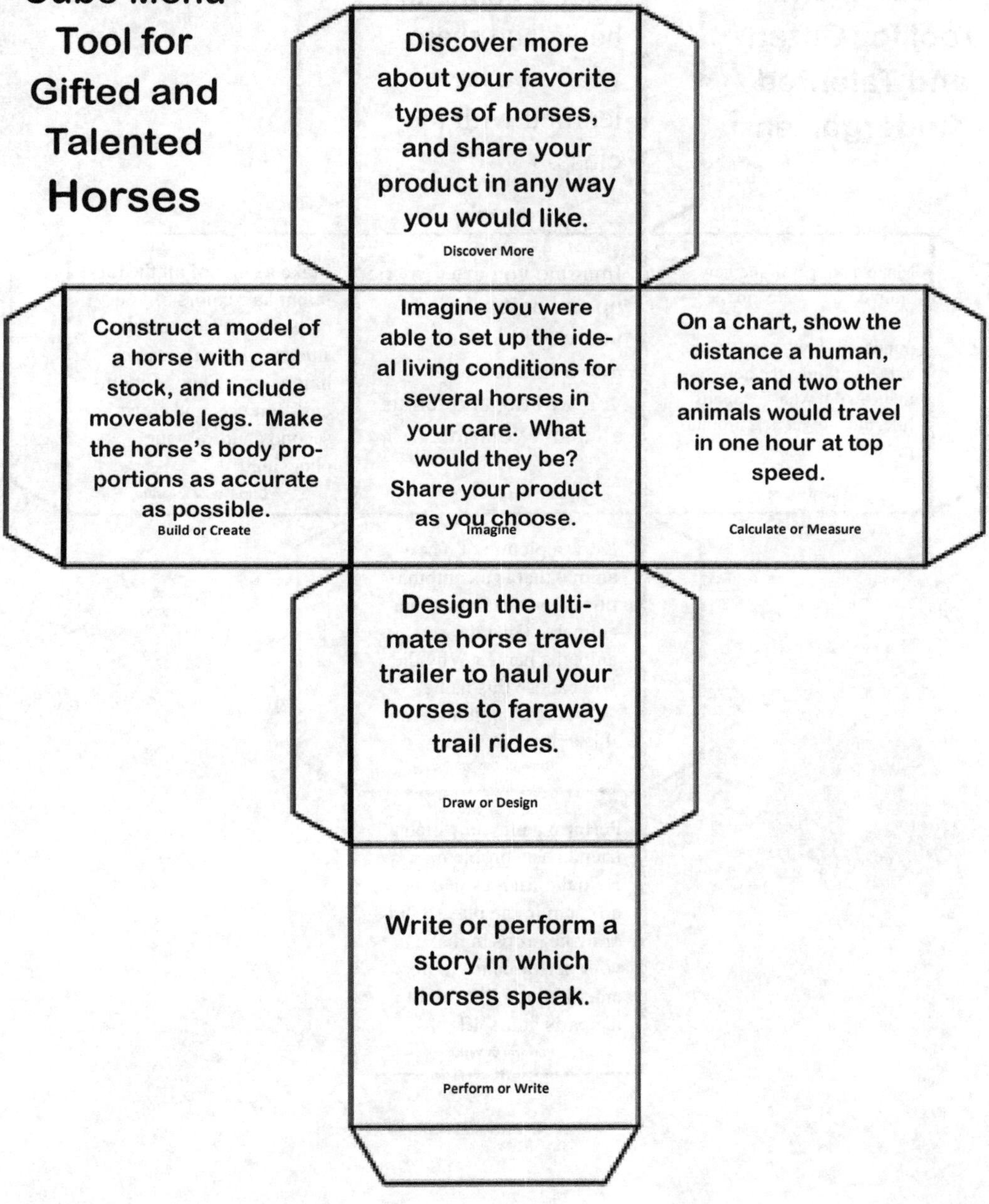

Discover more about your favorite types of horses, and share your product in any way you would like.
Discover More
Construct a model of a horse with card stock, and include moveable legs. Make the horse's body proportions as accurate as possible.
Build or Create
Imagine you were able to set up the ideal living conditions for several horses in your care. What would they be? Share your product as you choose.
Imagine
On a chart, show the distance a human, horse, and two other animals would travel in one hour at top speed.
Calculate or Measure
Design the ultimate horse travel trailer to haul your horses to faraway trail rides.
Draw or Design
Write or perform a story in which horses speak.
Perform or Write

Cube Menu Tool for Gifted and Talented Kindergarten

Read a nonfiction book, and share what you have learned with the class.

Discover More

Make a puppet of the new animal you created in the draw or design box. Use the puppet to show us all of the amazing things the new animal can do, what it sounds like, and how it acts around people.

Build or Create

Imagine you are grown up and doing the job you would love to do. Show us the things you will do, and tell us all about your job.

Imagine

Make a chart of all the different hair colors of your classmates. How many students share the same hair color? Choose another difference, and create a second chart of your choosing.

Calculate or Measure

Draw a picture of a new animal that is a combination of two or three other animals. Give the new animal a name. Why did you choose this name? What amazing things can this animal do?

Draw or Design

Perform a play in which a friend has a problem. Help the friend solve the problem in the play. Find or make props to make your performance more entertaining. Play all of the parts yourself!

Perform or Write

Cube Menu Tool for Gifted and Talented Math

Use a textbook from the next grade level or online tutorials to learn a new math skill. Create problems for a classmate to solve, and teach each other your new skill.

Discover More

Build three dimensional structures using paper and tape which will be placed in a miniature town. Make sure the buildings are sized properly in relation to one another. If you want, place the buildings on the map created in the "Calculate or Measure" square.

Build or Create

Invent your own tool for measuring flat, round, or uneven surfaces. Show another person the proper way to use the tool.

Imagine

Draw a large map for an imaginary town. Include a key on the map to show different distances. If you can, use the measuring tool invented in the "Imagine" square instead of a ruler or measuring tape.

Calculate or Measure

Design a secret code or math puzzle for your friends to solve. Send them a secret message or challenge them to solve your puzzle. Maybe you could create a game along with it!

Draw or Design

Create a performance which teaches the class how to do one of these things: adding fractions, multiplying, dividing, finding perimeter, or finding area.

Perform or Write

Cube Menu Tool for Gifted and Talented Non-Fiction

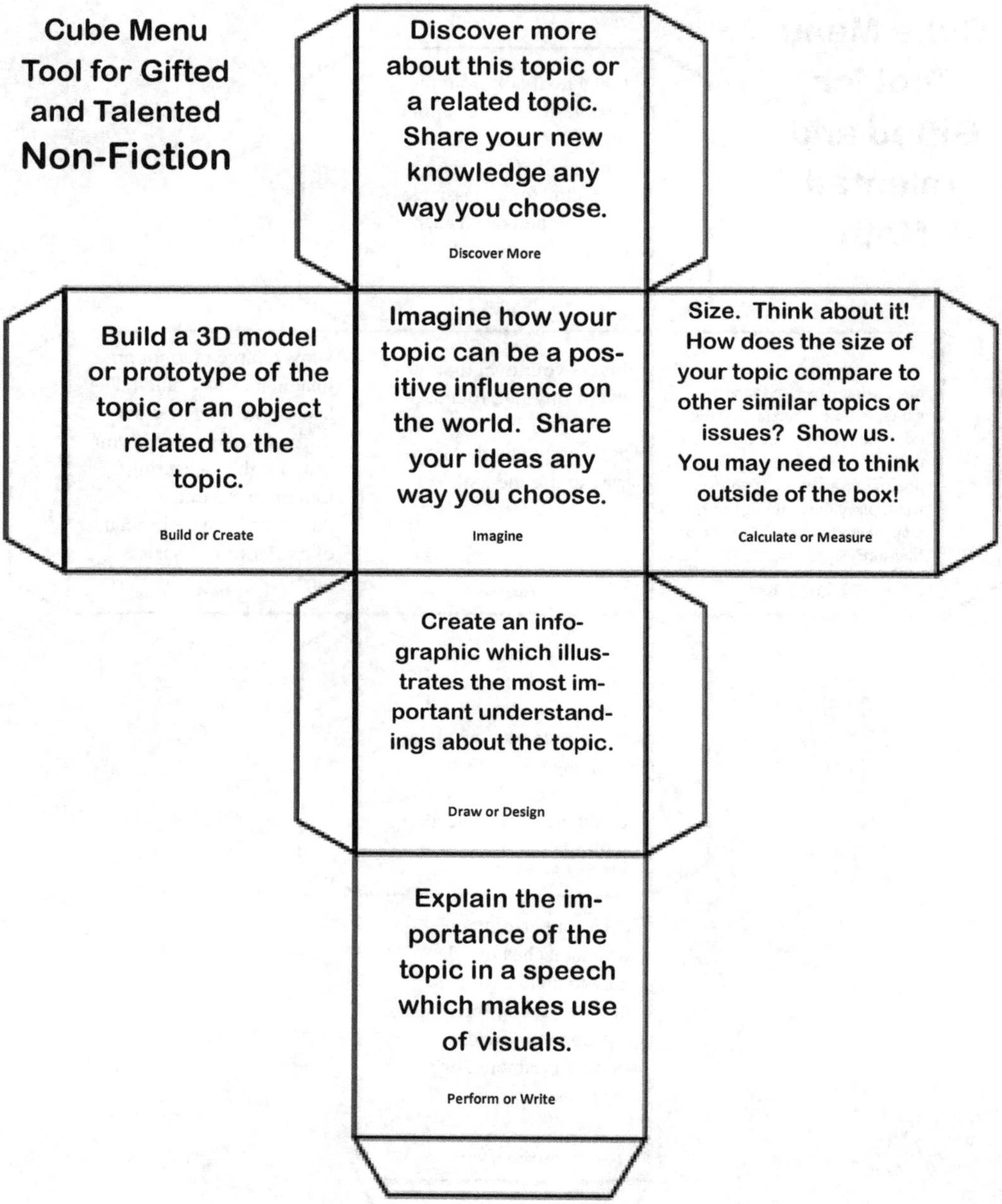

Discover more about this topic or a related topic. Share your new knowledge any way you choose.
Discover More
Build a 3D model or prototype of the topic or an object related to the topic.
Build or Create
Imagine how your topic can be a positive influence on the world. Share your ideas any way you choose.
Imagine
Size. Think about it! How does the size of your topic compare to other similar topics or issues? Show us. You may need to think outside of the box!
Calculate or Measure
Create an infographic which illustrates the most important understandings about the topic.
Draw or Design
Explain the importance of the topic in a speech which makes use of visuals.
Perform or Write

Cube Menu Tool for Gifted and Talented Poetry

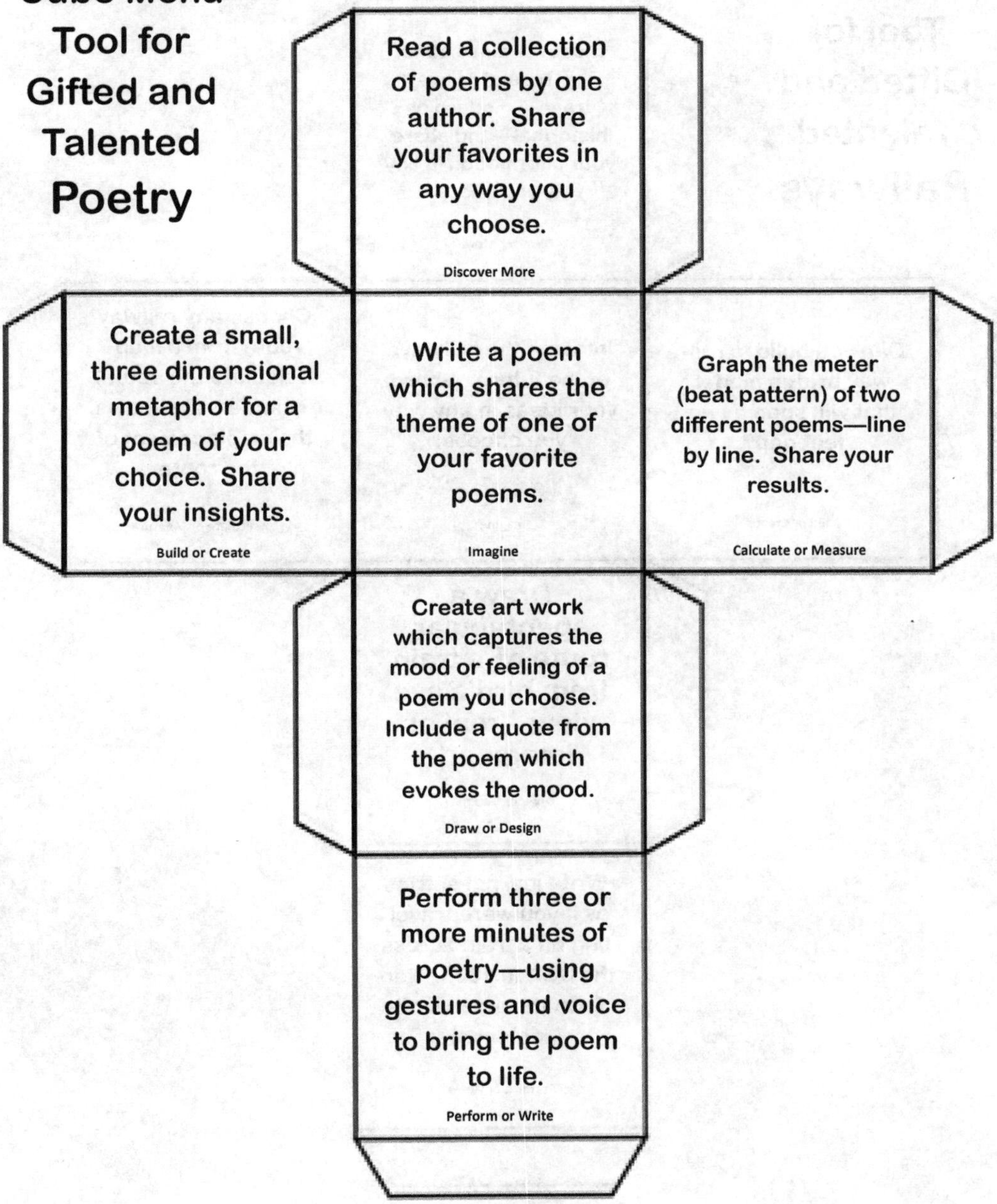

Read a collection of poems by one author. Share your favorites in any way you choose.
Discover More
Create a small, three dimensional metaphor for a poem of your choice. Share your insights.
Build or Create
Write a poem which shares the theme of one of your favorite poems.
Imagine
Graph the meter (beat pattern) of two different poems—line by line. Share your results.
Calculate or Measure
Create art work which captures the mood or feeling of a poem you choose. Include a quote from the poem which evokes the mood.
Draw or Design
Perform three or more minutes of poetry—using gestures and voice to bring the poem to life.
Perform or Write

Cube Menu Tool for Gifted and Talented Railways

Discover more about any type of railway travel—modern or historical—and share your information in any way you choose.

Discover More

Can you build a rail-way bridge model that will span a two feet gap?

Build or Create

Imagine the railways of the future. Share your ideas in any way you choose.

Imagine

Choose any railway route from a map. Calculate the actual distance travelled vs. the displacement of the route.

Calculate or Measure

Draw a spectacular route of a train from bird's eye view—real or imagined.

Draw or Design

Write journal entries as if you were travel-ling on a train across the USA in 1885. Per-form the most excit-ing event.

Perform or Write

Cube Menu Tool for Gifted and Talented

Social Emotional

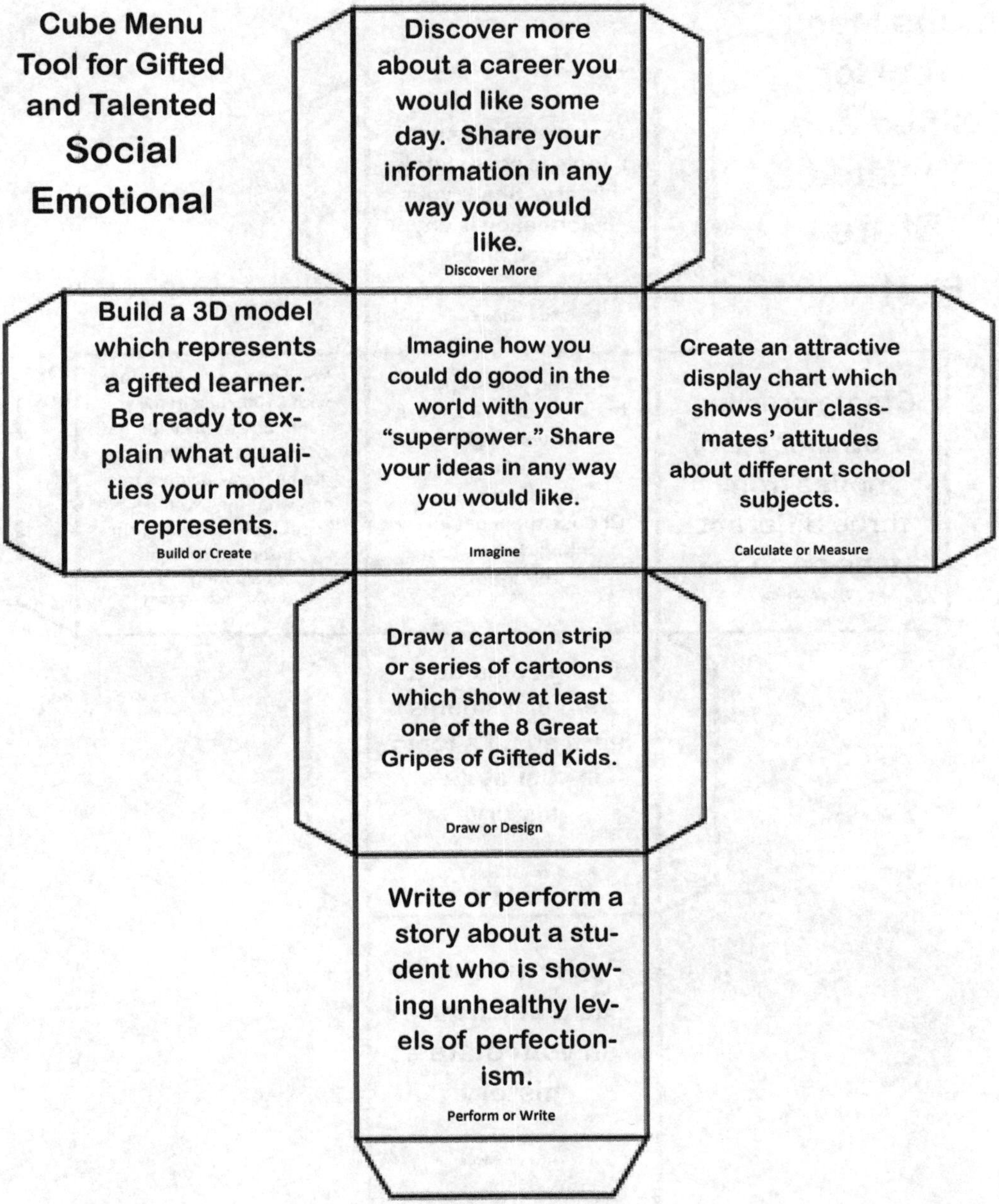

Discover more about a career you would like some day. Share your information in any way you would like.
Discover More
Build a 3D model which represents a gifted learner. Be ready to explain what qualities your model represents.
Build or Create
Imagine how you could do good in the world with your "superpower." Share your ideas in any way you would like.
Imagine
Create an attractive display chart which shows your classmates' attitudes about different school subjects.
Calculate or Measure
Draw a cartoon strip or series of cartoons which show at least one of the 8 Great Gripes of Gifted Kids.
Draw or Design
Write or perform a story about a student who is showing unhealthy levels of perfectionism.
Perform or Write

Cube Menu Tool for Gifted and Talented State History

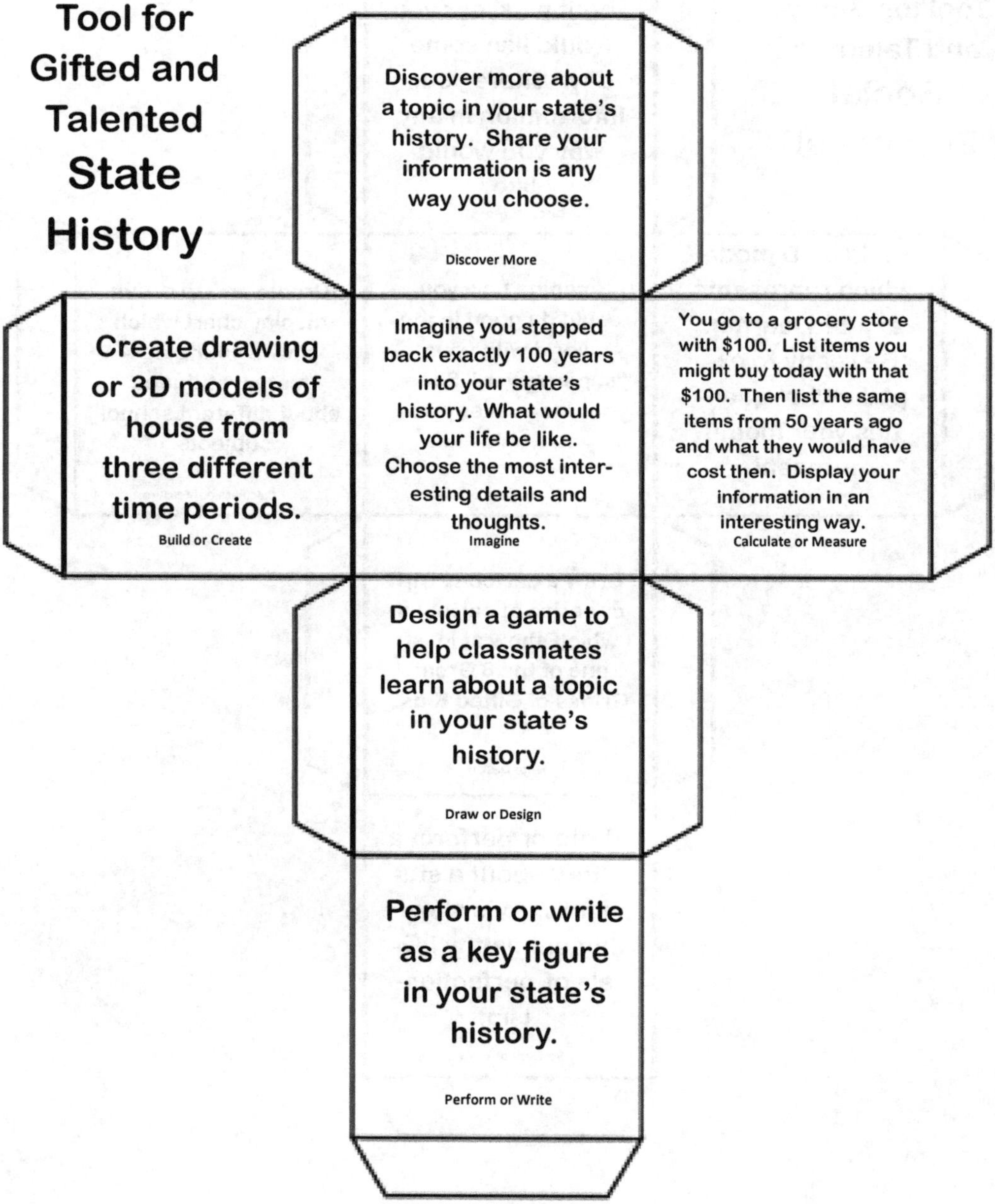

Discover more about a topic in your state's history. Share your information is any way you choose.
Discover More
Create drawing or 3D models of house from three different time periods.
Build or Create
Imagine you stepped back exactly 100 years into your state's history. What would your life be like. Choose the most interesting details and thoughts.
Imagine
You go to a grocery store with $100. List items you might buy today with that $100. Then list the same items from 50 years ago and what they would have cost then. Display your information in an interesting way.
Calculate or Measure
Design a game to help classmates learn about a topic in your state's history.
Draw or Design
Perform or write as a key figure in your state's history.
Perform or Write

Cube Menu Tool for Gifted and Talented USA Geography

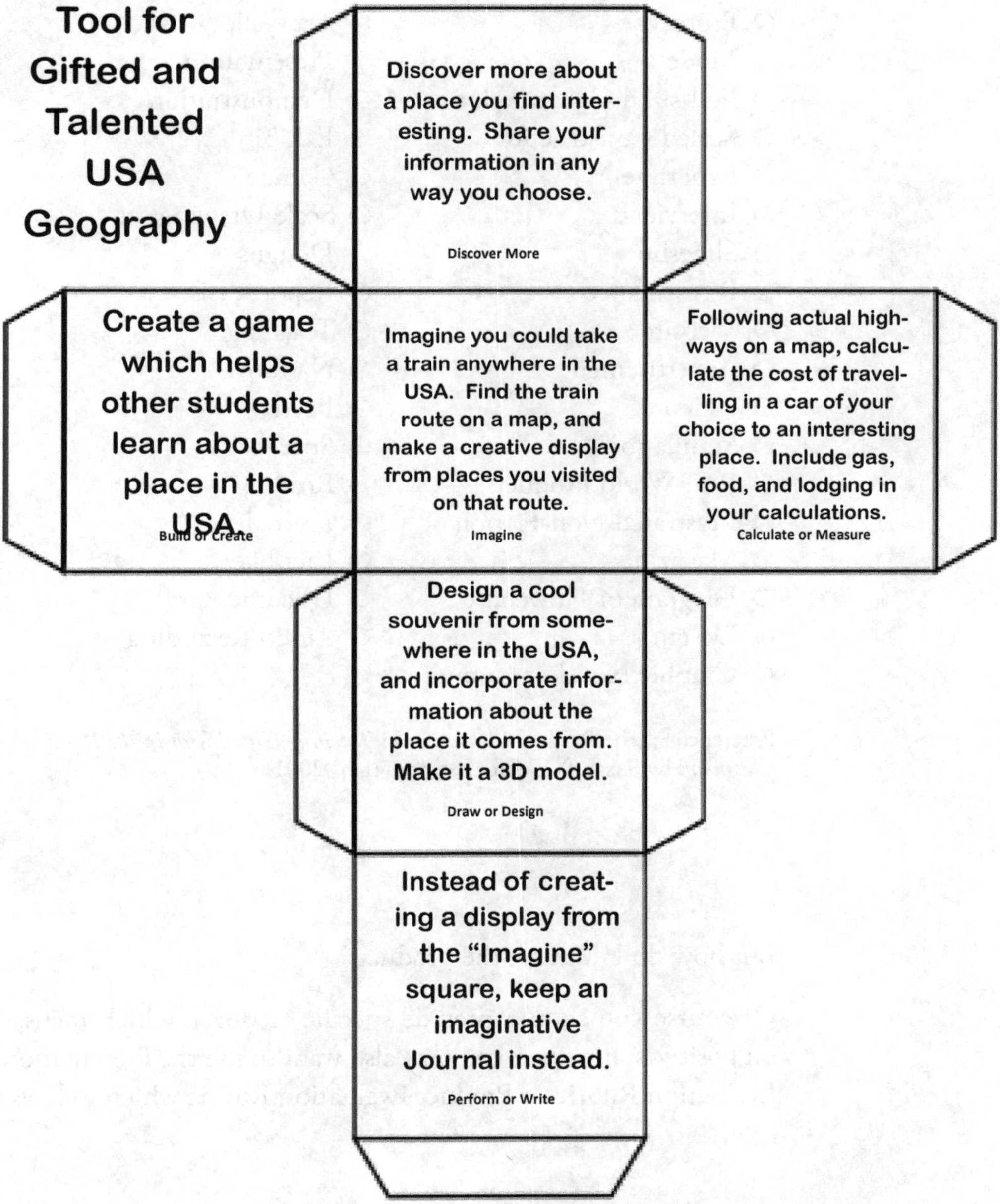

Discover more about a place you find interesting. Share your information in any way you choose.
Discover More
Create a game which helps other students learn about a place in the USA.
Build or Create
Imagine you could take a train anywhere in the USA. Find the train route on a map, and make a creative display from places you visited on that route.
Imagine
Following actual highways on a map, calculate the cost of traveling in a car of your choice to an interesting place. Include gas, food, and lodging in your calculations.
Calculate or Measure
Design a cool souvenir from somewhere in the USA, and incorporate information about the place it comes from. Make it a 3D model.
Draw or Design
Instead of creating a display from the "Imagine" square, keep an imaginative Journal instead.
Perform or Write

When we ask students to share what they know in any way they choose, this opportunity opens up vast possibilities for their response:

- ❍ Survey, Data, and Display
- ❍ Prototype
- ❍ Model
- ❍ Full-sized Construction
- ❍ Scaled Construction
- ❍ Experiment
- ❍ Interviews
- ❍ Slideshow
- ❍ Performance
- ❍ Website
- ❍ Advertisement
- ❍ Video
- ❍ Simulation
- ❍ Real-World Product
- ❍ Illustrated Non-Fiction
- ❍ Magazine
- ❍ Diagram or Flowchart
- ❍ Design
- ❍ Graphic Novel or Comics
- ❍ Brochure
- ❍ Art Gallery with Presentation
- ❍ Demonstration
- ❍ Exhibit
- ❍ Game
- ❍ Scale Drawings and Designs
- ❍ Report or Essay
- ❍ Teaching
- ❍ Narrative
- ❍ Poetry
- ❍ Speech
- ❍ Reading
- ❍ Journal
- ❍ Fact File
- ❍ Documentary
- ❍ Audio Recording

Reference for the Product Ideas Above: *Teaching Gifted Kids in the Regular Classroom* by Susan Winebrenner, copyright 2001

But how do I evaluate the products?

Of course you should provide specific feedback which focuses on positives; however, you may also want to use the Presentation Evaluation Rubric or Product Evaluation Rubric which follows.

Presentation Evaluation Rubric

Specific requirements for this presentation: What question(s) must be answered? What problem must be solved? What skills must be demonstrated?

Advanced	Proficient	In Progress
• Specific requirements for this product have been exceeded. • The audience is never in doubt as to when transitions between points are made. • Exceptional speaking and presentation qualities noted below: ☐ Details are clear and topic does not stray from main points. ☐ Main points are clear and reinforced. ☐ Volume is used effectively and/or strategically. ☐ Vocal variety both entertains and reinforces main ideas. ☐ Language and word choice are colorful and clear. ☐ Visual aids are used. ☐ We feel both informed and entertained. ☐ Sense of humor. • The presentation contains more detail or variety as compared to similar presentations of same-aged peers.	• Specific requirements for this product have been met. • Transitions are present between points. • The presentation does not stray from the topic; sufficient details are presented so that main points are supported. • The presentation contains an acceptable amount of detail or variety as compared to similar products of same-aged peers. • Vocal variety is used so that the audience is encouraged to listen. • Voice volume is sufficient. • Topic specific vocabulary is used when necessary. Word choice is clear.	• Requirements for this product are missing or incomplete and noted below: • The presentation's purpose design remains unclear throughout. • The presentation seems incomplete or off topic. • Essential details are missing. • The main points are undeveloped or under supported.

Notes:

Name________________________ Evaluator________________________

Product Evaluation Rubric

<u>Specific requirements for this product</u>: What question(s) must be answered? What problem must be solved? What skills must be demonstrated?

Advanced	Proficient	In Progress
• Specific requirements for this product have been exceeded. • The products stands alone. It needs little or no explanation or contains clear written explanations. • Exceptional design or artistic qualities are present and noted below: ☐ Attention to detail. ☐ Unique perspectives. ☐ Consistency of perspective or design. ☐ Expressions of abstractions like feelings, thoughts, and emotions. ☐ Poetic elements. ☐ Unique and/or creative combinations of elements. ☐ Combination of design and functionality. ☐ Metaphorical elements. ☐ Sense of humor. ☐ Multiple perspectives or other artistic skills. • The product contains more detail or precision compared to similar products of same-aged peers.	• Specific requirements for this product have been met. • The product's purpose and design is clear with explanation. • The product appears neat, complete, and attractive. • The product contains an acceptable amount of detail or precision compared to similar products of same-aged peers.	• Requirements for this product are missing or incomplete and noted below: • The product's purpose and design remains unclear even after explanation. • The product appears incomplete or lacks neatness. • Essential details are missing.

<u>Notes:</u>

Name____________________

Evaluator____________________

Using and Evaluating Student Products to Show Understanding

See the Slideshow all about Nurturing a Product-Based Classroom

https://www.teacherspayteachers.com/Product/Nurturing-a-Product-Based-Project-Based-STEAM-Classroom-FREE-Guide-2461026

About the Author

Mark Hess is President-elect of the Colorado Association for Gifted Students, and a board member and the editor of the SENG Library. He has published nine books for gifted specialists including 3rd, 4th, and 5th grade Gifted Social-Emotional Curriculums and the Hands-on Literacy, Critical Thinking series for 4th, 5th, and 6th grades. As Portable Gifted and Talented, Mark has shared over 25,000 free resources. You can visit his website at www.giftedlearners.org

CPSIA information can be obtained
at www.ICGtesting.com
Printed in the USA
JSHW011025151222
34800JS00007B/16

9 781953 360168